D0283838

## INAUGURAL EDITION

**SQ**

Sutherland Quarterly is an exciting new series
of captivating essays on current affairs
by some of Canada's finest writers,
published individually as books
and also available by annual subscription.

SQ

Twelve Days in London
**Funeral For
A Queen**

John Fraser

FORTHCOMING

SQ

The Story of the Convoy Commission
**An Emergency
in Ottawa**

Paul Wells

SUBSCRIBE
ONLINE
AT
SUTHERLANDQUARTERLY.COM

# FUNERAL FOR A
# QUEEN

# FUNERAL FOR A
# QUEEN

Twelve Days in London

JOHN FRASER

**SQ**

**SUTHERLAND HOUSE**

Sutherland House
416 Moore Ave., Suite 205
Toronto, ON M4G 1C9

First edition, December 2022

If you are interested in inviting one of our authors to a live event or media appearance, please contact sranasinghe@sutherlandhousebooks.com and visit our website at sutherlandhousebooks.com for more information about our authors and their schedules.

We acknowledge the support of the Government of Canada.

Manufactured in Canada
Cover designed by Lena Yang
Book composed by Karl Hunt

Library and Archives Canada Cataloguing in Publication
Title: Funeral for a queen : twelve days in London / John Fraser.
Names: Fraser, John, 1944- author.
Description: Series statement: Sutherland quarterly
Identifiers: Canadiana (print) 20220455767 | Canadiana (ebook) 20220455813 |
ISBN 9781989555903 (softcover) | ISBN 9781990823244 (EPUB)
Subjects: LCSH: Elizabeth II, Queen of Great Britain, 1926-2022—Death and burial. |
LCSH: Queens—Great Britain—Death. | LCSH: Monarchy—Great Britain.
Classification: LCC DA590 .F73 2022 | DDC 941.085092—dc23

ISBN 978-1-989555-90-3
eBook 978-1-990823-24-4

# ABOUT THE AUTHOR

John Fraser is a Canadian writer, academic, and founding president of the Institute of the Study of the Crown in Canada. He was editor of *Saturday Night* and a correspondent for *The Globe and Mail*. He is the recipient of multiple national journalism awards and was chair of the Canadian Journalism Foundation until 2008. He served as Master of Massey College from 1995 until his retirement in 2014. Also by John Fraser:

*Canada's Unemployed*
*Kain and Augustyn*
*The Chinese: Portrait of a People*
*Private View*
*Telling Tales*
*Saturday Night Lives*
*Eminent Canadians*
*Mad About the Bay* (with Elizabeth MacCallum)
*The Secret of the Crown*
*Stolen China* (fiction)
*The Master's Menagerie* (fiction)

This book is for the Guardians of the
Chapel Royal, Massey College

*Clara MacCallum Fraser*
*Principal Nathalie Desrosiers*
*Hon. Elizabeth Dowdeswell*
*Chief Stacey Laforme*
*Mary McGeer*
*Elder Carolyn King*
*Nathan Tidridge*
*The Rev'd Paul Wright*

And in memory of

*Georges and Pauline Vanier*

# CONTENTS

# DAY 1, THURSDAY, SEPTEMBER 8

This is an account of the death of a queen and the accession of a king. A straightforward story in some ways; complicated in others. It has been said of writers, perhaps cynically, that provided they begin and end their books well, it hardly matters what goes on in between. Is it the same for jobs? For marriages? For lives? For reigns?

What reign began better than Queen Elizabeth II's? In 1952, her principal realm, the United Kingdom, was still recovering from a devastating war in which it had shown itself undaunted, and after which it was economically crippled. At the time of her Coronation on June 2, 1953, eight years after the war's end, bomb damage was still widely evident throughout London and other large cities. The war-time hero and prime minister, Sir Winston Churchill, having been humiliated by electoral defeat in 1945 in what should have been his own finest hour, had scraped together enough votes to return to office, but he was a very old man and a spent force. Churchill's most useful purpose for the Coronation would be as physical contrast to a beautiful, vibrant woman who had only to wear the Crown jewels and ride sidesaddle for the annual Trooping of the Colour to leave most of her subjects star-struck and agog with admiration. She had the real man of her dreams, her prince, almost constantly nearby (albeit dutifully a few steps behind); her direct heir (Charles); and a spare (albeit a girl, Anne) in tow back at Buckingham Palace. A stupendous act of medieval pageantry loomed amid all the hopes and fears of a people and a world bone-weary of the previous half century of war and depression. Hope was the key word here. She was such a harbinger of hope and aspiration in those long-ago days, hope allied to a sense of duty, publicly pledged to last for as long as she might live. Oh yes, it began very well.

The Coronation itself, a year later on June 2, 1953, was a wonder to behold, even today when you can watch the whole three-hour marathon on egalitarian YouTube. It was the first to be fully televised and filmed. Having arrived in a golden coach, her mere procession *into* Westminster Abbey, preceded by some 250 church leaders, Commonwealth prime ministers, members of the Royal Household, civil and military poohbahs of all hues and descriptions, not to forget a sturdy flank of Yeomen of the Guard, dovetailed nearly three hours later by the procession *out* of the Abbey, remains one of the marvels of romantic ceremonial fantasy. How what was, in effect, just a fancy stroll down an aisle came to symbolize nearly a millennium of history and the power of illusion is something still to be wondered at.

And the ending nearly three-quarters of a century later?

It turned out better than anyone could possibly have imagined, better than any scriptwriter would dare, and almost too rich in imagery and consequence for the army of journalists sent to cover all the obsequies to adequately describe. Even the directors for the final episode of *The Crown* would be hard-pressed to reproduce something so incredible. How on earth did she manage to see off one prime minister and usher in a new one two days before she died? How did she manage to arrange her *envoie* in Scotland, the scrappy northern kingdom playing around with a possible independence referendum and thereby leave the architect of that strategy—the pushy Scottish First Minister, Nicola Sturgeon—as an almost embarrassing bit player in the funeral of the century? How did she confound each and every republican in all her realms with the reality of instantaneous hereditary succession even while they spluttered, *Of course, of course, she was a wonderful person and never did anything wrong, but now we must have that important conversation about the future of the monarchy,* even as the newly minted King Charles III vowed to maintain constitutional propriety as he effortlessly assumed all the perks and presumptions of his inheritance? Believers in the Crown and unbelievers alike were left shaking their heads in wonderment at what she pulled off in her final foray into the world her image so dominated.

Despite the fact that her death certificate claimed the Queen died of "old age," it had been rumoured in high circles for some months that she had been diagnosed with bone cancer and this was the source of her "mobility issues." If true, she and her advisers were adroit at keeping it secret right to the end and even into the grave, ensuring that the focus remained on a working sovereign, not a dying relic; focused on the pledge she made on her twenty-first birthday to serve "the people" for however long she might live.

Naturally there had been speculation about her looming death, simply because of her great age. You don't get to be ninety-six and famous without ending up on a media death watch. But it was surprising, and a sign of the magic the old Queen could still weave, how little journalistic speculation there was on the cause of the mobility issues. It was way more fun to follow Meghan and Harry. And especially Prince Andrew, that endlessly useful scarecrow.

She had lived to her unprecedented Platinum Jubilee. She had pulled a marmalade sandwich out of her ever-present purse to share a video moment of pure whimsy with Paddington Bear and endear herself to the whole damn world all over again. Whoever claimed the Royal Family doesn't know how to stage sideshows to keep the media at bay and the public well away from the main script never properly followed the long and glorious reign of that "Most High, Most Mighty, and Most Excellent Monarch, Elizabeth the Second, by the Grace of God of the United Kingdom of Great Britain and Northern Ireland and of Her other Realms and territories Queen, Head of the Commonwealth, Defender of the Faith, and Sovereign of the Most Noble Order of the Garter."

I am quoting her colourful and faithful minion, David Vines White, Esquire, Garter King of Arms, who recited all this after the late Queen's crown and scepter and orb had been passed on and her solid oak, lead-lined coffin was being lowered into the family vault below the sanctuary of St. George's Chapel in Windsor Castle. By that time, there were no more sideshows needed. Not for her reign at least.

She had pulled it off, perfect to the letter. The death in Scotland, followed by the leisurely procession of her mortal remains down the length of her most ancient realms, brought a massive outpouring of immense sadness, introspection, and gratitude, the immensity of which surprised only journalists and republicans. It wasn't really *grief*, either. *Grief* is the wrong word for anyone who has died while reaching, or nearly reaching, his or her century still in sound mind.

The manner of her passing said to all her realms that she was bigger than just England, bigger than anyone's contempt for hereditary principles, bigger than separatist sentiments not just in Scotland but also in Canada, in Australia, and even in Jamaica. Pictured two days before her death performing her constitutional responsibilities as she saw off one self-infatuated politician and welcomed another into The Presence really did seem in retrospect to have been scripted by herself. Even the last acts performed in her name both involved her "senior overseas realm"—that would be Canada—which she had troubled herself over all through her life

4

and over two dozen tours of one sort or another: the first last official act was a note of concerned condolence for Indigenous subjects killed and wounded in tragic multiple stabbings in Saskatchewan, one of her most loyal outposts; and the second, almost banal in comparison, was the signing of provincial legislation by her vice-regal appointee in the province of Ontario, her constitutional "stand-in," Lieutenant Governor Elizabeth Dowdeswell. When Ms. Dowdeswell brought the blotter up to dry off her signature, an aide leaned down to whisper in her ear that "Her Majesty has passed." In this case, it was the Queen of Canada who had passed, the sixth monarch since the Canadian Confederation of 1867, with the seventh already in place. She had been Queen for almost half the country's post-Confederation history.

Queen of Canada? *Canada?* Canada, Canada, Canada. Hardly mentioned on the day of her death yet so steeped in monarchical history most of its citizens have lost track of how it began and what exactly it means. It is lost in mists. Civic education is not one of the country's strong points, forever embracing as it does an echo culture from south of the border, a culture which, ironically, sometimes seems more infatuated with the Royal Family than the shivering masses north of the 49th parallel. Still, here were several members of the Royal Canadian Mounted Police, actually mounted, leading the funeral cortège. They were a tangible reminder that the Crown has been in Canada a very long time. It's factored into over a thousand place names, and into everything from Canada's court system and oaths of office right down to the favourite brand of Canadian whisky (Crown Royal).

Nearly two centuries earlier, for example, early in the summer of 1837, Anna Bromwell Jameson, wife of the Attorney General of Upper Canada, Robert Sympson Jameson, set off with Francophone voyageurs and Indigenous guides on an extensive trip along the shores of Georgian Bay, named after King George IV, who was in his youth an "interesting" mix: the Prince Harry and Prince Andrew of his day. She set off in what she thought was the reign of King William IV. A few days in, shortly after dawn, her large skiff neared Manitoulin Island, the largest island in the world on fresh water. Mrs. Jameson wrote in her famous account *Winter Studies and Summer Rambles in Canada*:

> There was deep slumberous calm all around, as if nature had not yet woke from her night's rest: then the atmosphere began to kindle with gradual light; it grew brighter and brighter; towards the east, the lake and sky were intermingling in radiance; then just there, when they seem glowing and flowing together like a bath of fire, we saw what seemed to us the huge black hull of a vessel, with masts and spars rising towards the sky—but we knew not what to think or believe! As we kept on rowing in that direction, it grew more distinct but lessened in size: it proved to be a great heavy-built schooner, painted black, which was going up against the lake against wind and current. One man was standing on her bows with an immense oar, which he slowly pulled, walking backwards and forwards; but vain seemed all his toil, for still the vessel lay like a black log, and moved not: we rode up to the side and hailed him.
>
> "What news?"
>
> And the answer was that William the Fourth was dead, and that Queen Victoria ruled in his place! We sat silent, looking at each other, and even in that very moment the orb of the sun rose out of the lake, and poured its beams full in our dazzled eyes.
>
> We asked if the governor were at Manitoulin Island? No; he was not there; but the chief officer of the Indian department had come to represent him, and the presents were to be given out

to the assembled Indians that morning. We urged the men to take their oars with spirit, and held our course due east by the woody shores of this immense island; among fields and reeds and rushes, and almost under the shadow of the towering forests.

Meantime many thoughts came into my mind—some tears too into my eyes—not certainly for that dead king who in ripe age and in all honour was gathered to the tomb—but for that living queen, so young and fair.

*"As many hopes hang on that noble head*
*As here hang blossoms on the boughs of May!"*

And what will become of them—of her! The idea that even here, in this new world of woods and waters, amidst these remote wilds, to her so utterly unknown, her power reaches and her sovereignty is acknowledged, filled me with compassionate awe. I say compassionate, for if she feel in the whole extent the liabilities of her position, alas for her! And if she feel them not!—O worse and worse!

I tried to recall her childish figure and features. I thought . . . she was not such a thing as they could make a mere pageant of; for that there is too much within—too little without. And what will they make of her? For at eighteen she will hardly make anything of them—I mean of the men and women around her. It is of a woman I think, more than of the queen; for as part of the state machinery she will do quite as well as another—better, perhaps; so far her youth and sex are absolutely in her favour, or rather in our favour. If she be but simple-minded, and true-hearted, and straight forward, with the common portion of intellect—if a royal education have not blunted in her the quick perceptions and pure kind instincts of the woman—if she had

7

only had fair play, and carries into business plain and distinct notions of right and wrong—and the fine moral sense that is not to be confounded by diplomatic verbiage and expediency—she will do better for us than a whole cabinet full of cut and dried officials, with Tallyrand at the head of them. And with what a fair heritage is this which has fallen to her! A land young like herself—a land of hopes—and fair, most fair! Does she know—does she care anything about it?—while hearts are beating warm for her and voices bless her—and hands are stretched out towards her, even from these wild lake shores.

* * *

Here's a handy side journey through the thickets of royal reportage to help you understand and interpret what you are reading. A short explanation first. When my father died in 1998, it fell to me to sort his library, where to my amazement I discovered he had more than a dozen biographies of Sir Winston Churchill, and that didn't include Churchill's own account of the Second World War and his autobiographical tome, *My Early Life*. I groaned, not from lack of admiration for the wartime leader but from my father's secret obsession, secret because he rarely talked about him, or at least not to me and my sister. Almost absentmindedly, I thumbed through some of these tomes: there was the one by Lord Moran, his physician, seen largely through Churchill's depressions or "black dogs"; there was Paul Reid and William Manchester's trilogy (*The Last Lion*) with its emphasis on the great man's intuitive genius and the American links coupled with the importance of the "special relationship" forged with President Franklin Delano Roosevelt; and so on. My father didn't live to see some of the revisionist anti-Churchill books, like Tariq Ali's *Winston Churchill: His Times, His*

*Crimes* but he would have bought them, too, although perhaps not for his library collection.

What is relevant here is that by thumbing through these books, I discovered almost more about the biographers than I did about the biographee. You can see the same phenomenon with the plethora of biographical essays and books about, say, the American poet Sylvia Plath, or Adolf Hitler, or Jesus Christ: they all take an attitude. Pop psychology is the common denominator, even in the academic or theological studies, and consequently you learn just as much, or more, about the messengers as you do about the subjects.

Magnify this tenfold when you are reading anything about British royalty. The range goes from obsequious adoration to the most scabrous, outraged anger. Let me sketch briefly ten degrees of authorial attitudes and you can make your own judgment about what you are reading, the book in your hands included. In no particular order:

1. *Mystical, obsessive reverence* from attendant preachers and worshippers of the Anglican cult of Charles the First, King and Martyr

2. *Craven sycophancy* from the editors and "journalists" of *HELLO!* magazine

3. *Colourful admiration* from Marion Crawford, the former royal nanny and author of *The Little Princesses*, and all other authors of "confidential" and allegedly insider accounts

4. *Respectful embrace* from essayists in *The Spectator* such as columnist and former editor Charles Moore; the Royal Canadian Geographical Society's CEO John Geiger; *National Post* columnist Chris Selley; and me in this book

5. *Balanced but edgy tolerance* from Tina Brown in her new book, *The Palace Papers,* and the publisher of Sutherland House and this book, Kenneth Whyte, in his newsletter *SHuSH*

6. *Hypocritical (but lucrative) neutrality* from most royals reporters for the English media, especially anyone writing on the late Princess Diana, like Andrew Morton, or the mawkish U.S. biography maven Kitty Kelley

7. *Tolerant indifference* from many prime ministers of Westminster-style realms, until they reach high office when, like Canada's Stephen Harper, they discover how useful a hereditary monarchy is, but also peer deeply into all the "head of state" alternatives which hugely scare them

8. *Negative indifference* from Canadian and Australian journalists who are constantly nonplussed by the continuation of a constitutional monarchy in their countries (in Canada this would be the hat trick of Jeffrey Simpson, Andrew Cohen, and Geoffrey Stevens, who have been assuring us for years that the death of Queen Elizabeth will begin the constitutional "great reset")

9. *Impatient irritation* from sophisticated know-it-alls like the late Hilary Mantel, *Wolf Hall* author, and novelist-essayist Will Self; also all the for-hire left-wing Brits who have given up trying to persuade the unwashed British public of the induced infantilism engendered by the Royal Family, but have now found a handy outlet for their wares with the *New York Times*

10. *Intemperate and obsessive outrage* from contemporary Robespierres and Tricoteuses like U.S./Nigerian linguistic academic Uji Anya, who took time out at the end of the Queen's life to note that "the chief monarch of a thieving, raping genocidal empire is finally dying. May her pain be excruciating."

Take your pick. If you belong to category 10, I would stop reading now and get busy with tumbrel construction. You never know when your moment might come along.

* * *

Outside the entrance gate to Balmoral Castle on the day that Queen Victoria's great-great-granddaughter died, the floral tributes had started. They would be laid or strewn in her honour all the way from the Highlands of Scotland to the vault below St. George's Chapel in Windsor Castle where, eleven days later, she would be laid to rest beside Prince Philip, her husband of seventy-four years, as well as her sister, Princess Margaret (make that Princess Margaret Rose to cover the earliest years of their lives together), and their parents, King George VI and Queen Elizabeth (the "Queen Mother" in her widowhood). About the last sounds to be heard at her obsequies at Westminster Abbey and St. George's Chapel were from her faithful Pipe Major of the Royal Regiment of Scotland, Paul Burns, who for some time had been her piper of choice to wake her each morning when she was in summer residence at Balmoral Castle.

But before all that could happen, there were still ten days of official mourning to be conducted according to the strictest of plans, all worked out years before and approved by the Queen herself. Nothing was to be left to chance, which was why the death in Scotland was such a boon: although it was listed as a possibility in the plans, it hadn't been fully prepared for because of an apparent presumption that there would be plenty of advance notice. Even the Queen's personal bodyguards in Scotland, the Royal Company of Archers, had been caught off guard and had to scramble to get their bows and quivers ready, which they did all the way down to the great hall in the Palace of Westminster. But the stage was set for a monumental farewell to begin and by dying so adroitly, the central figure in this drama had ensured everything could be set in motion appropriately and exactly on time. As she always did.

# DAY 2, FRIDAY, SEPTEMBER 9

By Friday morning, the blank spaces in the planning had been filled in, although Queen Elizabeth had been dead for barely half a day. Already the great transition was occurring, so quickly that her son and heir Prince Charles had become King faster than an ardent republican could say, *Now just hold on a minute!*

Republicans are an odd lot, just as odd as fervent monarchists. According to a recent *Guardian* study of the phenomenon, in both Britain and realms like Canada and Australia, actual card-carrying republicans are quite few in number and for reasons I can neither explain nor fully understand, largely restricted to middle-aged men. It could be constipation, looming impotence, or mere lack of imagination. Whatever. The faithful republican whose moment was supposed to have come when the dear old Queen finally died, found himself hearing "God Save the King" even before some newspapers had landed with the news that Elizabeth was no more.

Within days, the new King would be pictured at his desk with the famous red boxes containing the monarchical homework. A new royal cipher would be published along with the first profile images that will appear on the coins of his realms. *Whoosh*. Just like that! He and his Queen Consort would also do their first walkabout in front of Buckingham Palace to greet the early crowds. Camilla looked a little fragile and uneasy with her new role, but warmed to it in time. He looked like a pro. The people they greeted seemed grateful but also slightly bemused that they were directly in touch with the big changes. It was an unusual and interesting moment, as though both sides of this particular equation were dipping toes into uncertain water.

From the constitutional monarchist's point of view, the best thing about hereditary royal succession is precisely the speed with which it occurs. No opportunity for doubts to creep in; no doubts about who is to step up. The son famously had been waiting longer than any previous heir for his chance at the throne. Charles, in fact, was such a well-known entity that those opposed to the continuation of a monarchy in any form had thoroughly convinced themselves that the mere thought of him on the throne would set off an avalanche of critical activity and constitutional initiative which would inevitably result in the Crown's demise. But that didn't happen. There wasn't time.

That didn't mean there weren't issues to deal with, at least in some people's minds. We had better get the bad stuff out of the way first. Yes, his first marriage, to Diana Spencer, was a disaster. He was caught out trying to please too many people and ended up disappointing everyone. Yes, he can be stubborn, especially when a cause he has championed is questioned. Yes, he drives some people bananas when he publicly lectures them on architectural banalities, on conservation, on eco-farming, on climate change, on industrial waste, on the environment in general and on every particular of the environment. Yes, he's been around a very long time waiting for his moment, which has finally come in his eighth decade of hearing people sing "Long live our gracious queen."

He may have gnashed his teeth at that phrase, but somehow I doubt it. Throughout the new King's long sojourn as Prince of

13

Wales, a position for which there is no instruction manual nor any particularly useful precedent to follow (although a number to avoid), he had considerable freedom compared to the constitutional straitjacket into which he will now be locked. The causes he fought for, some of which he actually won (respect for Indigenous voices, for example) and some for which he was initially mocked but helped shepherd into our consciousness (climate change, most notably) will have to be handed on to his heir and other family members if substantial speaking out is required. Now he has to show that he can handle the frustration of being politically neutral and emotionally steady, neither his natural bent, but he is a surprising man in many ways and he still has a lot of time to surprise us.

On this day, the first full day of his reign, he made his inaugural address to his far-flung subjects and he managed it well. In fact, very well. He respected the narrow ideological parameters the throne imposes. He reminded us that people are greater than their press clippings and that they can evolve over time. "As human beings," he once said, "we suffer from an innate tendency to jump to conclusions, to judge people too quickly and to pronounce them failures or heroes without due consideration of the actual facts and ideals of the period."

There's a precedent in history here. King Edward VII was the son and heir of Queen Victoria, who ruled seemingly forever throughout much of the nineteenth century and left her name on the age. He came to the throne when he was into his seventh decade, along with some bad luggage including mistresses by the score (one related to King Charles's second and current wife), embarrassing legal tangles and court appearances, and a well-documented eagerness for indulgences in food and wine. No one thought he would amount to much of anything, yet he turned out to be an excellent constitutional monarch who was hugely responsible for the success of a critical diplomatic coup in the Franco-Britannic "Entente Cordiale" in which France and England ended a thousand years of often bellicose rivalry.

Charles is someone many people *think* they know only too well. They are sure he will fail as king, but their conviction is based almost exclusively on years of press reports, many of which have used Charles to make sport with a rollicking good yarn about a "royal," or to undermine the idea of a hereditary monarchy. Through it all, he not only maintained the proverbial stiff upper lip (well, occasionally it trembled), but also, he never abandoned the causes that mattered to him. He knew that his tenure as Prince of Wales would be his only chance to make a personal difference, as opposed to the symbolic difference he would be restricted to once he ascended the throne.

But if you doubt the interior grit of Charles Philip Arthur George to do the job he was born to do, do yourself a favour and type the following phrase into your search engine: *Prince Charles Australia assassination attempt 1994*. Watch his reaction as two shots are fired in his close proximity and a slow-moving policeman bumps him out of the way. Watch the ensuing melee and Charles's body language, and then listen to the opening comments he makes in his speech once the dust and chicken feathers have settled to the ground. If you don't think this is someone who was bred to be a leader, king or otherwise, then you deserve to have your republic.

Other indications of what kind of king Charles will be have been sprouting all over the place, particularly since his mother's retreat from active duty in late 2021 as health issues and encroaching infirmity slowed her immense energy and undermined her stoical sense of duty. He, too, has a sense of duty and service, different from hers but nevertheless palpable. King Charles is set to show the world that he can make good on the solemn oath of service he made over half a century ago when he was formally declared the Prince of Wales and heir to a unique inheritance which spans the globe. But it will be a different concept of duty and stoicism than was Queen Elizabeth's. For sure, he will engage people more fulsomely, laugh more openly, and share grief more movingly than Queen Elizabeth. That's just in his observable nature. Maybe—no, *probably*—and under certain kinds of pressure (think surreptitious photographers or pesky media interviewers), he will also show irritation more openly than his mother ever did. He is, after all, Prince Philip's son, too.

We already know he wants a more slimmed-down monarchy, but somehow I don't think it will be reduced to Scandinavian simplicity. There is just too much historical weight attached to the particular throne this particular king must sit upon and the British, along with their tourist industry, will insist upon a measure of colourful ceremony. He won't disappoint. In addition to having been something of a rebel throughout his long apprenticeship, he is also a traditionalist.

About that long apprenticeship. Look at all the way stations of his life: shipped off to a rough-and-tumble boarding school in northern Scotland, about the last place in the world he would have chosen for himself, but he survived it; spied on relentlessly by the local, national, and international media so that even a surreptitious cherry brandy became front-page news, but he laughed it off; every woman he ever dated was subjected to relentless media exposure, but in the end he succumbed to someone else's notion of duty and married, for him, the wrong woman; even with the "other woman" he deeply loved and eventually was able to marry, he has had to withstand media onslaughts most of us would have shriveled up and died under; he has been a good father and as many good parents discover, you can't always get the child to grow up the way you want. Through it all, Charles kept his course when almost anyone else would have said *Screw this, I'm off . . .* Through it all, he supported his mother; tried to support his errant brother, Andrew; tried to figure out how to support Harry on the loose and under the spell of his lady and "liberty"; tried to show that the monarchy, curious institution that it is, was fit for the times and its evolved constitutional responsibilities.

Consider also that Prince Charles is one of the most notable victims of tabloid media excess, and yet he has endured. That is as key as anything to understanding what a great king he will probably be. He endured not with a halo, for sure, but as a real human being who is heir to the failings all human beings are heir to, except in his case they have been displayed before the entire world: moments of triumph, moments of grief, moments of joy, moments of terror, sadness, and humiliation, moments of quiet resolution, and moments of vindication. My God, he even lived long enough to hear about women who were actually touched and moved by his notorious (and secretly recorded and broadcast) desire to be Camilla's tampon.

And there's this interesting conundrum. Although Charles's relationship to Canada is not as close as his mother's was, it's also not that far off and it's for reasons unique to Canada. He has toured the country officially nearly twenty times, not including a number of private visits for one cause or another. But the nature of those visits was always different than Queen Elizabeth's. He made a particular point of supporting causes that were close to his heart, none more so than Indigenous survival and reconciliation in a country which until very recently tended to shrug at meaningful support of First Nations. He saw wisdom in Indigenous ways, courage in their survival, and in a strange and perhaps inapt way, a kind of fellow victimization in being taken for granted. He grows Indigenous-sourced tobacco on his properties so that he can make appropriate gifts to Indigenous leaders who visit and consult him. In his own person, he is a vehicle toward reconciliation. His own foundation, the Prince's Trust Canada, has made support for Indigenous projects one of its fundamental goals.

So when, on the first day of his new life, he pledged to serve all his subjects regardless of their backgrounds or beliefs, with "loyalty, respect and love," he meant it. It doesn't mean he won't sometimes find himself treading in dangerous territory. It also doesn't mean the relentless scrutiny of the press and social media won't be joyfully trying to inflict as much embarrassment and contempt as some of its particular parts love doing. And we haven't even got to "Inkblotgate" yet. *Ink what?* (You have to wait for the sixth day.) On his first full day, it was enough that the new King, after such a long and patient wait, reassured a bereft populace and a number of nervous governments that he knew how to play by the rules of the game.

Once he had accomplished all that, Queen Elizabeth's faithful subjects could get on with the business of examining their own lives set against the endurance of an unprecedented seventy-year reign. The growers of flowers could get ready for one of the most extraordinary floral deluges in history, far greater even than the one for Princess Diana's funeral in 1997. In the British House of Commons, fourteenth prime minister, Boris Johnson, dismissed merely three days earlier, stood in his newly found backbencher place and found the eloquence that might have kept him in office if he hadn't been such a chancer. He called her "Elizabeth the Great," his best try at launching a historic brand to parallel Russia's Peter or Catherine. He began almost pianissimo (for him):

This is our country's saddest day. In the hearts of everyone of us there is an ache at the passing of our Queen, a deep and personal sense of loss—far more intense perhaps than we expected.

In these first grim moments since the news, I know that millions and millions of people have been pausing whatever they have been doing, to think about Queen Elizabeth, about the bright and shining light that has finally gone out. She seemed so timeless and so wonderful that I am afraid we had come to believe, like children, that she would just go on and on.

Wave after wave is rolling across the world, from Balmoral—where our hearts are with the Royal Family—and breaking far beyond this country and throughout the great Commonwealth of nations she so cherished and which cherished her in return. As is so natural with human beings, it is only when we face the reality of our loss that we truly understand what has gone. It is only really now that we grasp how much she meant for us, how much she did for us, how much she loved us.

When I think of the void she leaves, we understand the vital role she played, selflessly and calmly embodying the continuity and unity of our country. We think of her deep wisdom, and historic understanding, and her seemingly inexhaustible but understated sense of duty. Relentless though her diary must have felt, she never once let it show, and to tens of thousands of events, great and small, she brought her smile and her warmth and her gentle humour—and for an unrivalled seventy years she spread that magic around her realms.

This is our country's saddest day because she had a unique and simple power to make us happy. This is why we loved her. That is why we grieve for Elizabeth the Great, the longest serving and in many ways the finest monarch in our history. It was one of her best achievements that she not only modernized the constitutional monarchy, but produced an heir to her throne who will amply do justice to her legacy, and whose own sense of duty is in the best traditions of his mother and his country.

Though our voices may still be choked with sadness we can say with confidence the words not heard in this country and her other realms for more than seven decades:

God Save the King.

In an aside during this speech that isn't in the official account, Boris Johnson also paid tribute to her sense of fun, recalling a short promotional video in which she had starred:

She knew instinctively how to cheer up the nation, how to lead a celebration. I remember her innocent joy more than ten years ago after the opening ceremony of the London Olympics when I told her that a leader of a friendly Middle Eastern country seemed actually to believe that she had jumped out of a helicopter in a pink dress and parachuted into the stadium.

# DAY 3, SATURDAY, SEPTEMBER 10

Although Queen Elizabeth principally resided in Buckingham Palace, the royal court is formally based in St. James's Palace. It is home to some lesser royals and a setting for occasional official receptions. Until this week, most people didn't know that it also retains a crucial ceremonial function. The Accession Council meets in St. James's Palace in the event of the death of a sovereign, and the new monarch is proclaimed by a Great Officer of State, the Garter King of Arms, from the palace's Proclamation Gallery, overlooking Friary Court. Most people didn't know this because there hadn't been an Accession Council in seventy years. In all that time, the Proclamation Gallery has done little but collect dust.

The Accession Council consists of Privy Counsellors of the United Kingdom, the Great Officers of State (the Lord High Steward, the Lord High Chancellor, the aforementioned Garter King of Arms, etc.), the Prime Minister, and the Lord Mayor of the City of London, among others. Today it will do its ceremonial best to the accompaniment of a ninety-six-gun salute from the cannon at the Tower of London.

The colourful ranks of the College of Heralds, part of the Royal Household—the name given to all those who work to serve the sovereign—has been seen from time to time during the seventy-year reign of Elizabeth II, but never in such profusion, never in all their glory with their beautiful if semi-ridiculous tabards of silk embroidery, nor with the trumpet fanfares from the raised gallery overlooking the great forecourt of St. James's Palace. Most of the time the heralds are invisibly overseeing pedigrees, coats of arms, the flying of flags, and such. On this day, they will have the honour of reading the formal proclamations of the Accession Council.

You would have to be nearly eighty years old to remember the proclamation of a new British sovereign, and even then you would have seen it in black and white. And for those same eighty-year-olds for whom singing "God Save the Queen" seemed so strange back in 1952, much of the world on this day found it weird to hear "God Save the King."

St. James's Palace dates back to the reign of Henry VIII in the sixteenth century. That extraordinary pack of Royal Heralds goes back even earlier, to the fifteenth-century reign of Richard III. The current oaths of office for a reigning monarch are rather newish and Hanoverian (i.e., eighteenth century), tied as they are to legislation guaranteeing the succession of a willing and confirmed communicant in the Church of England. The oaths have been adjusted to accommodate the changing times. No longer can the inheritance of the Crown bypass a first-born who is a daughter, ending nearly a millennia and a half of male primogeniture. And an heir of whatever sex can now marry a Roman Catholic, or a Muslim, or a Hindu, or an atheist, so long as the heir him- or herself maintains the link to the official Church of England. But considering what the Church of England condones these days, it hardly matters.

The wheel of history moves on, retaining and restructuring as it goes. The whole remarkable second full day of the new sovereign is rooted not just in the realities of current times, but also in delightful if occasionally murky history and a jumble of mythology about kings and queens and knights in shining armor, in triumph and tragedy, in duplicity and also in service, soaked in both ceremonial froth and vengeful blood. I could go further and bring in King Arthur and the Round Table (the model for King Edward III's creation of the Most Noble Order of the Garter in the fourteenth century), but the point is that the Crown is hedged in by both mystery and mysticism as well as by *realpolitik* and fragile validity. King Charles III was already discovering what his mother knew so well: you have to run very fast in order to stay in the same place, and forbearance in most things is the actual rule of the day. All of this mélange was on view on the second day of mourning.

The fact that Charles became king the very second the last breath left his mother's lungs is acknowledged on the day but the theatre of accession is designed to make sure everyone else knows it, too, including the representatives of all the other realms of which the Queen was head of state and the King is now. So in they all came, governance and legislative leaders, archbishops, high commissioners, and ambassadors from far away, and not for once forgetting the Lord Mayor of London, who is very zealous to protect his historic precedence in the scheme of things. They all listen to the announcement of the death of the Queen, the proclamation gets signed by the appropriate hands, and everyone bundles into the next big room and waits for the object of all this arcane but necessary activity to arrive and agree to take on the honour and burden of kingship.

The sense of the moment is not so much grave as expectant. It all seems so new, or at least so little known. Yet it is also ancient and has been performed many times over the centuries, even if not for the better part of a century since the accession of Elizabeth II. And then the central actor, the new king in his eighth decade, simply appears. He walks through a doorway, bows slightly and stiffly to the assembled grandees of the realms, and then mounts a lofty dais festooned with all the gold and scarlet magnificence of royalty surrounding the vast throne of all his realms—flummery, some might call it, and Charles, wisely, treats it all nonchalantly. He spoke these words:

> I am deeply aware of this great inheritance and of the duties and heavy responsibilities of sovereignty which have now passed to me. In taking up these responsibilities, I shall strive to follow the inspiring example I have been set in upholding constitutional government, and to seek the peace, harmony and prosperity of the peoples of these islands and of the Commonwealth realms and territories throughout the world.

Who talks like that in this day and age? Who evokes the Lord God Almighty for guidance and help? How on earth has this survived the era of social media, toxic attacks on those who would set themselves high, and the levelling of all things sacred and esteemed? To employ the great Canadian put-down, who does he think he is?

But he does it well. Very well. Maybe he has survived to this extraordinary moment because he is linked to our common heritage to make something more of life than a mere passage of time, to link ourselves to ancient things, to venerate aspiration, to elevate even a very contemporary divorced father of two to a certain nobility that is hard to define but is tied to the same commitment to service the old Queen evoked most of her days on earth. You could remember her and now look at him, and see through the mists to that same beautiful aspiration.

Or not. You could also, like the British novelist Will Self, see the whole thing as a sign of willing infantilism. Take your pick, but while you decide, note that Elizabeth Alexandra Mary has safely and brilliantly begun her epochal journey to the grave and her son Charles Philip Arthur George has just made an equally safe journey onto the very throne she left behind. Just by walking through that door. Nothing more, and everything else.

# DAY 4, SUNDAY, SEPTEMBER 11

Today was the day the Queen's earthly remains, already in that lead-lined coffin of solid oak, were transported a hundred miles from Balmoral Castle to the Palace of Holyroodhouse in Edinburgh, seat of Scottish monarchs, home of the Scottish regalia of crown, sceptre, and sword, and site of all the Scottish investitures. In one of the great quirks of history, Queen Elizabeth died a Presbyterian (the state church in Scotland of which she is titular head) and would be buried an Anglican (because she is the titular head of the Church of England).

The whole Scottish adventure seemed designed by the late sovereign to underscore that her reach extended well beyond Buckingham Palace in central London. The spectacle unfolding north of Hadrian's Wall transfixed the world as they saw scenes enacted in places that didn't look at all like Piccadilly Circus or even England. There were kilts and bagpipes and accents as sweet as heather.

She surely must have foreseen and, I suspect, been quite pleased at this small coup. Like the one she once pulled on her formally tolerated but unloved British prime minister, Edward Heath. That was in August 1973, just prior to a gathering in Ottawa of the Commonwealth Heads of Government. It was well-known that Heath resented the Commonwealth, that he thought it kept British minds off the important goal of joining the European Common Market (as it was then called). He also knew very well constitutional tradition and the requirement that the Sovereign accept the advice of her First Minister. Just as he did two years earlier at another Commonwealth Heads of Government gathering, in Singapore, he advised that the Queen not go to this Canadian gathering in Ottawa because of the continuing and "unacceptable" presence of Idi Amin, the Ugandan president and despot. This time, the Queen was on to the game. She trumped Heath by calling another First Minister, Pierre Elliott Trudeau, and asking his advice. Unsurprisingly, he advised her to come. Since Trudeau was the official host First Minister, he trumped the "secondary" Heath and the Queen had forced her disgruntled British PM to backtrack. I heard subsequently from Esmond Butler, Private Secretary to Governor General Roland Michener, that the Queen was almost unctuous in making sure Mr. Heath felt comfortable in "her Canadian home."

So the Scottish setting for her final *envoie* unfolded almost on cue. What hadn't been scripted was that behind the hearse with its glass-encased viewing interior came an escort vehicle transporting the Princess Royal, who stayed close to her mother from the moment she died in her bed. Princess Anne became an extraordinary talisman through the official days of mourning. She took on the mantle of every individual subject who felt himself or herself there beside that coffin, following it down the highways and byways of Scotland, past fields with their early autumnal crops or lying fallow from prior reaping, past grazing cattle and cars stopped on the sides of roads in respectful attendance, under arching bridges crowded with Scots folk who wanted to make their farewells. She was still at her mother's side when at last they arrived at Holyroodhouse, the place Queen Elizabeth visited every year in July to preside over garden parties and meetings with Scottish leaders before hightailing it up to what for her was the sheer bliss of Balmoral Castle and all her highland rambles.

When the hearse reached Holyroodhouse, the Princess Royal was already out of her escort car and ready to receive the coffin as it passed by her through the entrance to the palace, carried by eight stalwart and kilted members of the former Argyll and Sutherland Highlanders Regiment (now subsumed into the Royal Regiment of Scotland). As it passed, the Princess Royal did a deep court curtsy to her mother and that act alone, done by the most independent-minded female by far in the entire Royal Family, made a significant impression on the millions watching. She curtsied for all the daughters of worthy and well-loved mothers the world over. She curtsied for men who couldn't even understand what a curtsy was. It was a public act of love and deep respect rendered personally and also on behalf of the public and it hit all the way home into the hearts of anyone who witnessed it.

* * *

The planning for the Queen's death had included the possibility that she might die in Scotland. It had to, obviously. She spent much of the summer there every year and the contingency planning had its own code name, "Operation Unicorn," which was an add-on to the overall plan known as "Operation London Bridge." That 400-plus-page document had been leaked to the media a couple of years earlier. As a still-functioning journalist, I don't believe in accidental leaks. They mostly happen for a reason. There would have been detailed plans for the death of Elizabeth almost from the day she ascended the throne. Assassination is always a threat.

So are accidents. From way back when, so much of the panoply of a monarchical system is tied to ceremonial observances and, save for a Coronation, nothing is as transfixing as the state funeral of a sovereign: not a baptism nor a wedding, not a Jubilee nor a solemn thanksgiving after a war. *Nothing* quite matches the grave import and solemnity of a state funeral for a sovereign, presided over by an heir. It is the defining moment in the very notion of hereditary monarchy and it is designed to do two things, hopefully brilliantly: be a focus of personal sadness and reflection for millions of people who are enabled to set their own lives beside that of their sovereign; and also be a form of shock and awe, displaying the symbolism and grandeur of the personification of the state.

That's why advance planning is so important. I have no doubt they are working on, or updating, King Charles's funeral plans even as you are reading this. The "they" in this case all report to the senior peer of the realm, the Duke of Norfolk, whoever it might be of a day. That's what dukes of Norfolk do: they manage the great moments in the lives of sovereigns and the nation. This particular duke was christened Edward Fitzalan-Howard and he is the eighteenth holder of the title since King Richard II created it in 1397. He shadowed his father at great state events to learn the ropes, just as he was shadowed at this period of mourning by his son and heir Henry Fitzalan-Howard, who holds the title of Earl of Arundel.

Curious trivia point: the young Earl of Arundel's surname, like his father's, includes "Fitzalan," and the "Fitz" has an interesting history. Up until the reign of Charles II in the latter part of the seventeenth century, it simply meant "son of," but Charles II had many illegitimate children to whom he gave the distinguished-sounding surname of "Fitzroy," or literally "bastard son of the king." So now you know. There is no question about the legitimacy of the current Earl of Arundel, I hasten to add, even if his mother and father at the time of the funeral were caught up in a messy divorce. Members of the Royal Family have been doing divorce since 1533 when Henry VIII dispatched Queen Catherine of Aragon in favour of Anne Boleyn. You could say that the entire Reformation history of the Church of England, and thus of the worldwide Anglican communion, rests on a divorce case. That doesn't make it better or worse than the Church of Rome, which is built on its own historical double standards, or than any other denomination, but it's always useful to be aware of particularities.

\* \* \*

If Norfolk *père et fils* got their jobs through heredity, like the old Queen and the new King themselves, the same cannot quite be said for the Scottish guardians of the person of the sovereign, the Royal Company of Archers. I say "quite" because heredity can sometimes be a factor. The Royal Archers have often passed along their duties from father to son. You probably noticed them throughout the week, in Scotland and later in London. They were the ones dressed like an upmarket version of Robin Hood and his Merry Men, with bows and quivers at the ready and their jaunty Balmoral bonnets festooned with a soaring eagle feather (or two or three feathers depending on rank). In Scotland the Royal Archers perform much the same function as the Yeoman of the Guard in London: they are ceremonial guardians of the sovereign's "person." They do have some degree of responsibility for basic protection, holding crowds back, for example, or keeping an eye out for "bad actors." Primarily, however, they are present for ceremonial purposes. The heavy lifting of personal protection is done by the professionals in the police service.

The history of the Royal Company of Archers is rich, with origins, like so much else on view this week, somewhat lost in the mists of time, when the longbow was the greatest weapon of war in Europe. The last battle on Scottish soil when a longbow was deployed to kill someone was in 1688 at the Battle of Mulroy. It was a clan dispute between the Camerons and the Mackintoshes. The Camerons won and the longbow left the battlefield forever, confined to sporting and ceremonial use. To this day the Archers hold annual archery competitions with prizes which reach back a couple of centuries in origin. They are also summoned each year for royal garden-party duty and during the preparations and the inspection, especially among some of the older members, the inspecting officer can sometimes be heard saying things like: *Straighten up, sir, and pull in your chin. That's right. And the second chin, too, sir, if you will.*

As with many Scottish traditions, much of what we get to see today comes to us courtesy of the romantic imagination of the Scottish novelist Sir Walter Scott. Although variations of the Royal Archers' services can be traced back many centuries, they did not emerge formally as an entity until the reign of Queen Anne, when they got their charter, and even then it needed a special push from Sir Walter, a century later, to set them on the road to being the official bodyguards of the sovereign. This was occasioned by the extraordinary state visit of King George IV to Scotland in August 1822, almost exactly two hundred years prior to the death of his successor, Elizabeth II. Much of what we associate with Scottish heritage today emerged almost full-blown, seemingly for the first time, from that visit, including the plethora of tartans and ceremonial kilts, with poetry supplied by Robert Burns (himself an Archer), and music from God only knows (composers' names tend to get lost). One year after the wildly successful royal visit, Sir

Walter wrote a novel (*Quentin Durward*) about a Scottish Archer who ended up in the service of King Louis XI.

To be an Archer, then, is an honour and you have to be a Scot, or be known to have strong Scots ties. And you have to be elected, whether you are the high-and-mighty Duke of Argyll, or a humble sheep farmer. I happen to know and have had a long friendship with a particular Royal Archer who is a retired sheep farmer from the Borders, those storied lands just to the north of the English border. My friend's son, who is now a businessman in London, was also elected an Archer and the two of them were both on duty for the late sovereign: Andrew, the sheep farmer in Edinburgh, and his son, William, in London at Westminster Hall.

A few years earlier, on a holiday with Andrew and his family, I ended up as his driver when he was called upon for the annual garden party at the Palace of Holyroodhouse in Edinburgh. Andrew didn't have a driver's licence and had to get to Edinburgh in time to muster for a practice drill. It was great fun to watch. These Royal Archers were not at all used to being regularly regimented; some were of a certain age, and of considerable girth. Their service is voluntary and mostly confined to garden party duty (although they are also seen at other select ceremonies presided over by the sovereign, including the annual service to honour members of the Order of the Thistle at St. Giles' Cathedral in Edinburgh).

Later at the palace on the day of the annual royal garden party, Andrew marched in with his fellow Archers and assumed protective positions behind which the assembled invitees waited to witness members of the Royal Family make their rounds. It's a rendered service similar to that of altar assistants at the Eucharist or Mass, performed out of respect for tradition and the desire to serve in however modest a fashion. It can come across as quaint or weird, but to many it is a tangible sign of tradition honoured and duty rendered, like so much else that happens at court. It certainly adds a distinctive Scottish embellishment to the progress of a reigning monarch, and also a departed sovereign.

Members of the Royal Company of Archers stood guard over the coffin of the late Queen from the moment her family handed it over to the state in Edinburgh, and they stayed with her all the rest of the way "home." In Westminster Hall, a week and a day later, I would watch William, son of Andrew the retired sheep farmer, twice mount the guard in his Archer's uniform at the catafalque. I have known William since he was a boy. He spent a summer with my family in Georgian Bay when he was seventeen and, more recently, I have been joyously jostled by his own sprightly children. The sight of him at such a solemn moment in such an extraordinary setting caught me completely by surprise and left me profoundly moved and in tears of pride mixed with almost inchoate sadness. In trying to catch as much as possible of the official mourning period for this book, I had not had time on my own to ponder what on earth I felt at the Queen's passing, at least not until then. Whatever the number of degrees of separation between myself and the remarkable events unfolding day by day, they seemed to vanish for precious seconds when William stood on guard for his Queen and my Queen and the Queen of all of us. Sir Water Scott would have understood and been quite pleased.

# DAY 5, MONDAY, SEPTEMBER 12

This was the day the royal drama took on almost cosmic significance as millions of people all over the world became caught up in the spectacle. The president of France made a solid point when he said Great Britain and her other realms had lost *their* Queen, but the rest of the world had lost "*the* Queen." He underscored a point rarely commented on.

It was Queen Elizabeth's lot to preside over the greatest sustained act of decolonization in history (there were still seventy British colonies and dependencies at the time of her Coronation and today there remain twelve territories clinging to colonial status at their own request, not Britain's). Yet it was one of her great achievements in those same years to have transformed her family into an *international* monarchy, recognized as special and unique not just in the realms like Canada and Australia, not just in the other Commonwealth countries that have adopted the republican system of government yet still regard the sovereign as head of the Commonwealth and an empathetic ally, but also to most of the rest of the world. It sometimes seems as though everyone, everywhere, is prepared to get caught up in any royal drama or ceremonial event with this particular family. In fact, no country gets more caught up in the glory and muck of royalty than the United States of America.

As morning dawned, King Charles and the Queen Consort were back in London preparing to meet a joint session of Parliament in Westminster Hall. In a few days, the hall would be transformed to receive the late Queen and one of the most remarkable tributes to any world leader would unfold as hundreds of thousands passed through the hall and past her coffin.

But at this particular moment, Charles's critical task was to speak the words parliamentarians needed to hear: that the new king was their servant, not their master, and that in the business of kingship he pledged to follow the example of non-interference established by his mother, and her father, and her father's father. And they had to take his measure just as he had to take theirs. He stood at a gilded lectern with the Speakers of both the House of Lords and the House of Commons on either side of him. Camilla attended, as well. Everyone was still adjusting not only to the new words for "God Save the Que—King," but also to the notion of "Queen Consort." It no doubt dawned on some that if his first marriage had worked out, Diana Spencer would simply have been Queen Diana, "consort" be damned. The newish title of "Queen Consort" is a tangible tribute to Diana's lingering presence. It can't last, though. Charles is too grateful to his consort to leave her with that title. She will be Queen Camilla soon enough.

The new King made an eloquent and adroit evocation of his mother's profoundly felt constitutional heritage:

> While very young, her late Majesty pledged herself to serve her country and her people and to maintain the precious principles of constitutional government which lie at the heart of our nation. This vow she kept with unsurpassed devotion. She set an example of selfless duty which, with God's help and hour counsels, I am resolved faithfully to follow.

And then he was off, Queen Consort in tow, back to Scotland to join the cortège that accompanied his mother's coffin in stately procession from the Palace of Holyroodhouse through the streets of Edinburgh to St. Giles' Cathedral for a solemn service of remembrance. St. Giles' is the great High Kirk of Scottish Presbyterianism where John Knox once railed against Elizabeth's ancestor Queen Mary. That would be the very same lady who her namesake, Elizabeth the First, ordered beheaded on July 24, 1587. The very same crown that had adorned that head before its severance nearly half a millenium before, was placed on Elizabeth II's coffin on this day in 2022. Such remnants of history are among the most important artifacts, physical and spiritual, in the story of monarchy. They *resonate* with anyone who chooses to embrace them.

* * *

The procession to St. Giles' was not entirely without incident, and there was a moment, probably inevitable, when Prince Andrew—the notorious Prince Andrew—was booed and called "a pervert." It was just a single boo followed by a couple of insults but it *resonated*, too, a reminder that the Royal Family has not only skeletons in its collective closet, but also some open sores. They were all on display during these amazing days, especially the continuing drama of Prince Harry and his troubled wife, who seems destined to become the Wallis Warfield Simpson of our times. You will recall Mrs. Simpson rescued King Edward VIII from the tedious rounds of royal duty and service, somewhat like Ms. Markle has rescued her prince. Harry looks both miserable and defensive in his decision, much like his great-great uncle, and he still has a lot of life to live with the consequences.

Scotland and other Scottish sensitivities were also *resonating* this day. The premier of Scotland, Nicola Sturgeon, a feisty bundle of worked-up independence mixed with curious insecurity, seemed reduced to minion status at the service in St. Giles'. It didn't help that the grandeur of the setting, even for Presbyterians, tended to dwarf her. She got to read one of the lessons and had primacy of position, but the drama and the evolving spectacle of the Queen's death, together with the growing realization of how vast the scope of mourning was, rather mocked her reading.

It was a famous reading, too, one of the Bible's best-known set of *push-me/pull-me* verses, from the Book of Ecclesiastes, chapter 3 in the Jewish scriptures ("A time to tear and a time to mend; a time to be silent and a time to speak," etc.). For Nicola Sturgeon, it was a time to lie low and a time to wonder why the Deity had chosen Scotland as the setting for this old Queen to die and her people to be taken up with such massive grieving, just as the premier was trying to get everyone's minds concentrated on her fight for Scottish independence. As Woody Allen once said, evoking Yiddish wisdom: "If you want to make God laugh, tell him about your plans."

\* \* \*

The image that was fixed in viewers' minds by the end this day was not that of the putative leader of an independent Scotland, but the Queen's four children all solemnly standing to attention with bowed heads and joined by the loyal Royal Archers around their mother's coffin: Charles, the dutiful; Anne, the faithful; loyal Andrew, the miscreant; and best-effort Edward, the afterthought. At this moment, their individual identities ceased to matter. They were all transformed into vigilant guardians and it seemed, somehow, right.

# DAY 6, TUESDAY, SEPTEMBER 13

The late Queen's coffin left St. Giles' Cathedral with the same ceremonial courtesies that attended her arrival, but somehow the courtesies seem to be getting more emotional. They would continue to build in intensity as the proceedings converged on London. In the meantime, the ancient Crown had been removed from atop the coffin before it left the cathedral and was returned to join the other "Honours of Scotland" (sceptre and state sword). Still attending upon her, the faithful men of the Royal Regiment of Scotland carried the bier down the cathedral's ramp to the waiting motor hearse which was to take the late Queen to Edinburgh Airport and the next part of the journey to Buckingham Palace for a day and a night, and the one chance the Royal Family had to be alone for some private grieving.

Another striking image that bore into memories of this day is those regimental Guardsmen in their kilts and their closely linked arms in the service of their sovereign. It was difficult to think that these same guards had been in combat in the Middle East not long before. As they grimaced a little under the weight of the lead-lined bier, you could not tell whether it was because of the weight of their burden or the solemnity of the occasion and the honour and pride they felt at carrying out such a solemn duty. Perhaps all of the above, but the particularities didn't really matter. It was extraordinarily moving and a sight rarely seen anywhere. It also matched perfectly the sense that for this Queen and her monumental death, it was wondrously appropriate. A constitutional monarch is said to be powerless in matters of state governance. It did not look like powerlessness on the steps of St. Giles'; it looked like a powerful conjunction of Then and Now twinned in a moment of global unity and coherence, a kind of heroic counterpoint to a different kind of global drama in the Ukraine where Russia's Vladimir Putin was able to occupy a diametrically opposite centre stage.

\* \* \*

As the coffin left the cathedral, as it headed for the airport, as it was loaded onto the air transport plane, as it landed in London, as it made its way to Buckingham Palace, the Princess Royal was never more than a few feet away.

\* \* \*

By the time the coffin had left St. Giles', King Charles and the Queen Consort were already in Belfast as part of the plan for them to visit every part of the ancient realm. In time, the other realms, from the vastness of Australia and Canada and New Zealand to tiny Papua New Guinea and Belize, will get similar royal treatment, but the first priority was to secure the home base, which Charles did brilliantly even with the looming scandal of Inkblotgate.

Every single one of Charles's movements during the ten days of official mourning was watched by his own special collection of unbelievers and trolls, which apparently includes a not insignificant part of the world media. The doubters are convinced that Charles is either a complete doofus or a ticking time bomb. They took up the chase with the official signing the previous week in St. James's Palace of the state documents supporting his kingship. A silver ink pot stand, donated by his sons, sat on the desk blocking the way of the state documents which had to be placed above the ink pot. In an act of apparently unprecedented and horrifying *lèse-majesté,* the new King grimaced and waved at an aide to move the ink pot to one side of the desk so he could write his name on the document.

*Aha! Voilà! Caught you!*

The media hounds and Carolean trolls had caught the scent. Imagine their joy when in Belfast and Northern Ireland this particular morning, the pen handed to Charles for the signing of the royal moniker leaked all over his hand and onto the page. Ink blots marred the pristine document and looked to all the world like a Rorschach test.

Let's analyze the new King's response first. Did he say *Damn this blasted thing* and hurl the pen across the room? No, he said, in effect, "I hate when this sort of thing happens," and in short order established a new rule that for the rest of his reign he would bring his own pen. But not before the *horreur* had been fully aired, analyzed, and picked clean for psychological implications. That's when the pop psychology got really interesting.

"King Charles has been seen airing his frustration during a ceremony for the second time in four days in Northern Ireland," blared *The Guardian.*

"Leaky Pen Sends Charles Over the Edge: 'I can't Bear This Bloody Thing,'" screamed the headline on America's *The Daily Beast.*

The most eloquent of the many other comments on all sides of the Atlantic and Pacific Oceans was by Sutherland House publisher Kenneth Whyte (publisher of this book and a chum from days of yore) in his popular newsletter *SHuSH* where he took up the vantage point of Tina Brown, who tagged Charles as "Eeyore" in her bestselling *The Palace Papers*. Whyte took a deep dive into Charles's psyche:

> As alarming as his incompetence is his temperament. He's had a lifetime of training for this moment—he's been waiting impatiently the whole of his seventy-three years for this moment—and when it arrives he's fuming over the positioning and performance of writing instruments in full view of his family, staff, and a global audience. His first move on noticing ink on his fingers? Hand the "bloody thing" to Camilla so it can leak over her hands. It made me wonder what kind of man we'll be singing for God to save.

As noted, there was more written in the same vein all over the place. Mercifully, Inkblotgate passed, refusing to travel further, at least this time. The extraordinary panoply of the late Queen's departure overwhelmed even such a universally followed newsletter as *SHuSH*.

Charles and his Queen Consort made it safely back to London to be on hand for the arrival from Edinburgh of the Queen's coffin. Somehow no one had thought to take him off in a straitjacket after that alarming exposure of alleged incompetence, rage, and humiliating self-exposure. But be warned and prepared as you watch the life of King Charles III unfold in the days and weeks and years to come: for the rest of his life, every expression of frustration or anger, and there will inevitably be a few, will cause Inkblotgate to reappear. Count on it, and when it happens ask yourself seriously if you still think, as my comrade Mr. Whyte may think, that Charles has been unfamiliar with this kind of pop-psychological potshot analysis all these past seventy years. Because he could get it, and got it, easily enough as heir to the throne, when his anger at climate change ignorance and his "childlike" belief in the wisdom of Indigenous voices were dismissed as obvious signs of his unreality and unfitness for the throne. You may end up thinking, like me, that he is the most resilient and decent public figure currently on the go in the topsy-turvy world we seem to have inherited at the moment.

\* \* \*

Although the quick trip to Belfast was a certain success, the wounds of the city and the territory remain. The Irish Troubles are not so far removed as the new King might have liked. Sectarian divisions remain between Protestants and Catholics, even now, a quarter of a century after Northern Ireland's 1998 peace agreement. For some, the monarchy is still an oppressive presence.

For Charles, Ireland is a reminder of a family tragedy when his beloved uncle and mentor, Lord Mountbatten of Burma, was assassinated. His mother had shown him an example of wary forgiveness, which she symbolized on her famous 2012 trip to Belfast, shaking hands with the Sinn Fein deputy leader Martin McGuinness, a former IRA commander. Charles said he felt deeply the significance of his mother's "shining example" in extending a hand "to make possible the healing of long-held hurts."

However, on Belfast's Falls Road, an Irish Nationalist stronghold, the healing hand fell ungrasped. This was the territory of Bobby Sands, the IRA terrorist who died in a British prison in 1981. "No, he's not our King," said an angry Bobby Jones, reported by the CBC. "Queen never done nothing for us. Never did. None of the royals do."

* * *

London was ready to receive the Queen. The city had seen her a thousand times in different times and places through the byways and broad thoroughfares, along the Mall, and on the way out of town to Windsor Castle. Pall Mall leads to St. James's Palace: all of its commercial windows had pictures of the Queen in them, but the crowning achievement in funeral decorations indisputably belonged to the Reform Club. Pall Mall is famous for its clubs, most of which go back to the end of the eighteenth and beginning of the nineteenth centuries, and the Reform Club is very special, partly because its membership was founded by and is still comprised of the kind of reformers who would have identified with the causes the new King champions, but also because of its architecture, inside and outside. Throughout the official mourning period, the Club was decked out in black mourning bunting from every window on its second floor. As far as I could learn, it had not been thus decorated since the death of Queen Victoria in 1901, when its windows were similarly draped. Inside, the vast and beautiful central galleria court, framed by a quadrangle of second-floor balconies—the high point of architect James Barry's 1838 design— was also disported in funeral garb. I've always loved the west wall above the galleria. It features three figures important in nineteenth-century Canadian political and social history: in the middle is a large portrait of Earl Grey, the grandfather of the Fourth Earl Grey who donated Canada's Grey Cup to the world of professional football; to his right is Lord Durham, who bequeathed Canada his Durham Report, which set the stage for self-government of the remaining North American British colonies; and on Earl Grey's left is a past Lieutenant Governor of Upper Canada with a title to die for but now sadly extinct: Lord Sydenham & Toronto.

The Club also featured a Platinum Jubilee exhibition in honour of the Queen. It was still on display as crowds unlike any seen for ages engulfed the city. London transport had to close down the entrances to the Green Park tube station because of the crush of people wanting to leave floral tributes near Buckingham Palace or just to stand by for long enough to say they had taken part. In one of the display cases at the Reform Club, almost inexplicable, was the christening gown of King Charles I in seemingly perfect condition. This is the same Charles I who was beheaded for "crimes against the nation," i.e., he thought he could stand in the middle of The Strand, or some other suitable thoroughfare, and murder someone without consequences . . . or was that another absolute ruler? It was an odd item to exihibit in the midst of Jubilee celebrations for Queen Elizabeth, but seeing it at the advent of the first sovereign brave enough to sport the name "Charles" since the death in 1685 of Charles II seemed somehow apt. Charles II was sometimes called "The Merry Monarch" for, in no particular order, he loved parties, actresses, flirty ladies, and wily courtesans, cocker spaniels, and unfettered bank accounts. He also managed to keep his head on his shoulders by adroitly confounding the predictions of his enemies, just as his namesake must do in the new Carolean era.

The crowds turned Green Park into a floral extravanganza in honour of the late Queen. Officials had got the hang of how to handle the massive tributes brought by the hordes of mourners. All the cellophane was removed and the bouquets were artfully placed around some of the great trees in the park, most of which had been planted during the reign of the second Charles. There was such a rush just to see the floral tributes that it became something of a crowd control ordeal in its own right. Fences had to be set up and in the near distance were dozens of porta-potties, proof that the authorizes are now accustomed to this kind of sudden and explosive public expression. Indeed, the porta-potty business was everywhere in evidence, not only near Buckingham Palace but also all along the queue that was starting to assemble days before the Queen's body arrived.

\* \* \*

Her coffin—make that *The* Coffin—arrived in London in the early evening, but a London early evening that was already dark and drizzly. The hearse brought it to a darkened Buckingham Palace where, despite the weather, crowds continued to swell. It was hard to tell exactly what was driving people to stand around in the damp cold. Of course, it was a sign of respect and also an attempt, however inchoate, to put oneself in the path of history, but there was something else that seemed to be animating the endless queues. Once again, people were putting their own lives up against that of the Queen's. "She was always there," was the almost constant chorus, usually followed by any number of "I"s, as in: "I was only ten when I first saw her wave from a car" or "I felt she brought warmth to the country," or "I knew that so long as she stayed on the throne everything would be all right," or "I thought she would live forever," or "I thought of her as family."

Were they grieving for themselves more than for the old Queen? Grieving for the lives they have thus far lived? Maybe not, but also maybe. It was hard to decipher, but the death of the sovereign was turning out to be not just an emotional watershed, but also a kind of personal reckoning. Strange, and also at times strangely moving. People were seeing themselves as part of something larger than themselves and it wasn't a country or even an institution—it was the frail frame of a ninety-six-year-old widow. She herself had become the embodiment of history and constitutional evolution.

She was old England, of course, but also a symbol of a newer and more equitable dispensation.

Ready to receive the coffin, even before the Royal Family assembled inside Buckingham Palace, was the Sub Dean of the Chapel Royal at neighbouring St. James's Palace. The titular dean is the Bishop of London, but it is the Sub Dean who does all the work and tends to the supervision and upkeep of all the Chapels Royal. There's the principal establishment at St. James's Palace, but there are also Chapels Royal at Hampton Court and a few other places, including one in Scotland, and, unusually, three in Canada. In this case, at the principal Chapel Royal at St. James's Palace, it is the Reverend Paul Wright who is in charge as Sub Dean. He is an official in the Royal Household, a servant of the old Queen and now of the new King. There had not been a coffin with a resting British monarch inside Buckingham Palace since the funeral of King Edward VII, and that was over a century ago, in 1911. The Sub Dean had to track down a photo of that earlier scene to see how it was done. On that occasion, it emerged, King Edward's coffin had been placed in the throne room, with a crown and orb atop, but no flag or personal standard draped over the coffin. There were four candles on raised stands at the four corners, in front of which stood four Grenadier Guards, their heads bowed and their rifles at rest. In place of a throne was an altar with cross and candles.

Much of what the world took in at the Queen's lying in state and funeral dates from the funeral of that same Edward VII, the Queen's great-grandfather. Her great-great-grandmother, the Queen-Empress Victoria had decreed no lying in state for her and her funeral was nearly a royal shemozzle—the horses that were supposed to haul the gun carriage bearing her coffin refused to co-operate and in the end 142 naval ratings (sailors) were required to pull (and brake) their burden from the train station in Windsor to St. George's Chapel. This started the tradition that we were to see again; it seemed rooted in ancient history but was in fact barely a century old.

Things went more smoothly for Elizabeth. Her family had this one chance to mourn her passing in private. As for the Sub Dean, he had been expecting this moment for a couple of weeks, ever since he had to cancel his visit to Canada where he was scheduled to meet with the only Chapels Royal outside of the United Kingdom, all three indicative of the Crown's special relationship with Indigenous nations, specifically the Mohawks of the Brantford area and the Mississaugas of the Credit River.

And it was in connection with those Chapels Royal in Canada that I had a small role to play in this vast drama, very small but one with huge resonances for the new reign. But that was to come on Thursday.

# DAY 7, WEDNESDAY, SEPTEMBER 14

The elaborate staging of the late Queen's obsequies—you can't just call ten days of ceremonial mourning "a funeral"—followed the rigid plan set out long before the actual event. It had been regularly updated to accommodate current circumstances, but pretty much following a plan that was built upon previous state obsequies throughout the past millennia and, as mentioned, took much of its current form since the reign of Queen Victoria. Having the sovereign's body lie in state in Westminster Hall, that extraordinary masterpiece of medieval architecture that has been at the centre of English, and later British, ceremonial and political life, seems encrusted in ancient tradition and ceremony, yet it has only been "traditional" since the death of Edward VII in 1911. It is the oldest part of what is called "the Palace of Westminster," which includes the Houses of Parliament, both Commons and Lords, and dates its foundation to 1097 under King William II, son of the Conqueror. According to the lore of the time, William's attendants told him they thought the new hall too big, too grand, and he hurled back at them that it wasn't half as big or grand as he wanted. Size is crucial if you're seeking to deploy shock and awe, and that is probably one of the reasons it was decided to bring Edward VII there before the actual funeral service at St. George's Chapel in Windsor Castle.

Queen Elizabeth was brought to Westminster Hall from Buckingham Palace after its day and a half of private mourning by the Royal Family, again following the precedent of her great-grandfather. In her case, she was accompanied for the procession down the Mall from the Palace, through Admiralty Arch and then on to the Hall, by her four children— the King, the Princess Royal, and the two spares, Andrew and Edward—each of them on foot. Behind them were four grandsons, William and Harry, Peter Phillips (son of Princess Anne), and the Earl of Snowden (son of the late Princess Margaret, the Queen's sister).

If you parse the drama of this remarkable week, you can see that the procession and the lying in state were all part of the buildup to the actual funeral service at Westminster Abbey. (Edinburgh had been the "dress rehearsal.") The calibration of it all was minutely designed, planned, and executed, and the effect, as intended, was pure magic: the precision of the Guardsmen who carried their heavy burden so loyally and lovingly; the music from the Gentlemen and Boys of the Chapel Royal as the coffin was borne in; the hush of the great hall as its history and grandeur wrapped itself around the catafalque; the stoical grief of the family; the great officers of state—prime minister, cabinet, Archbishops of Canterbury and York and the other prelates and leaders of different denominations and religions, the Earl Marshal himself with his baton of office, and all the Gentlemen Officers of the Royal Household—all reduced to bit parts. Glimmering atop the coffin, in case anyone forgot what the whole business was about, was that extraordinary symbol of monarchy, the Imperial State Crown.

Especially the crown! Can we pause for a moment here and consider its particulars. Although it has existed in various forms since the fifteenth century, it actually was only "built" in its current incarnation in 1937 for the Coronation of the Queen's father,

George VI. It is actually the "working Crown," used for the annual opening of Parliament, for example, and not the larger St. Edward's Crown which was the one placed on her head, and on the heads of all the Kings and Queens of England, at their coronations going back to Charles II in 1660.

I was rehearsed on the specifics of the Imperial State Crown by my Glaswegian granny in 1953 in the lead-up to the Coronation. She lived with us in Toronto and I was nearly nine, a perfect age to be inculcated in all things royal and fantastical. The crown is made with gold, silver, and platinum, with a velvet interior cap trimmed in ermine and festooned—what other word could you possibly use—with 2,868 diamonds, 273 pearls, seventeen sapphires, eleven emeralds, and five rubies. Some of the gems have stories all their own: there's St. Edward's sapphire, taken from the ring of King Edward the Confessor when he was reinterred in the Abbey in 1163; there's the Black Prince's ruby from the fourteenth century; the Stuart sapphire from the seventeenth century; and three pearls that once belonged to and adorned the first Elizabeth in the sixteenth century.

Once the coffin was properly placed, the crown was joined by two other earthly manifestations of the monarchy, those twin sisters, the orb and sceptre. The sovereign's orb is the symbol of God's power over all the earth. Less spiritually, it was made in 1661 for Charles II after the restoration of the monarchy following England's experiment with republicanism. It has its own lineup of precious stones, but it is essentially a hollow gold sphere adorned with a cross.

If the orb is the sign of God's wideness in the world, the sceptre is the specific sign of the monarch's actual power. It looks very much like a descendant of a brutal battle instrument, somewhat calmed with the help of the world's largest diamond, the Cullinan 1, also known as the First Star of Africa. It was given to Edward VII by the old Dominion of South Africa to help continue reconciliation after the ugly business of the nineteenth-century Boer wars. It will be handed over to King Charles at his Coronation in Westminster Abbey, most likely by the same Archbishop of Canterbury standing before the coffin in Westminster Hall on this day. He will say to Charles:

> Receive the rod of Equity and Mercy. Be so merciful that you be not too remiss; so execute justice that you forget not mercy. Punish the wicked, protect and cherish the just, and lead your people in the way wherein they should go.

But this will be months down the road. Right now, the miles-long queue of people are patiently waiting their turn to pay their respects once the Royal Family departs. All the specifics of what has been planned for this stage of the obsequies have been carried out to the letter. The Royal Family are off the hook for a few days and it is time for "ordinary" people to pay their respects, and so they will do without break over four days, more than a quarter million of them, including the world-famous footballer David Beckham, who stood in line for four hours and seemed to enjoy the illusion that he was ordinary, hampered only in this goal by the number of people wanting his autograph. He did manage to clamp down on selfies as inappropriate.

# DAY 8, THURSDAY,
# SEPTEMBER 15

I started the day with a cup of coffee back at the Reform Club, still looming over Pall Mall in its magnificent mourning clothes. It seemed a good start for a walk up to Piccadilly and then for a rendezvous in Green Park, adjacent to Buckingham Palace, to check out the growing extravaganza of floral tributes to the Queen, which were attracting worldwide attention. The rendezvous was with Lisa LaFlamme, the former anchor of Canada's leading news broadcaster, and this itself is a bit of a tale.

A journalism friend, I had watched Lisa's rise within CTV, the largest of the Canadian private broadcasters, with edgy admiration. Edgy because she had been chosen over another friend who I thought would get the gig. He thought so, too, but was instead brutally expunged. I had come to see CTV's top brass as stupidly cruel in the way they handled these promotions and demotions. The years pass and despite having got CTV news to the very top of the ratings game, and being widely admired across the country, Lisa was given her marching orders in what seemed an act of meanness and misogyny by a youngish CTV broadcasting executive trying to show "who's in charge here." The fallout was ferocious and although it didn't get Lisa her job back, it sent the creep, who apparently didn't like the fact that she let her hair go its natural, and very stylish, grey, on an unwanted departure "to spend more time with his family." Lisa had recently come to blows with the executive over CTV's coverage of the Platinum Jubilee. He wanted to downplay it. "She's our Queen, too," she had reminded him.

So Lisa LaFlamme is a hero of mine and she was now footloose in London, having taken an assignment with another Toronto-based broadcaster with a national cable affiliation to cover the funeral. She had asked me to join her to provide commentary on the air on the day of the funeral. She is a dream to work with and I was glad to say yes but this day, the Thursday before the Monday funeral, we were just wandering around, looking at the floral tributes piling up in Green Park, and working out some arrangements for the upcoming broadcast.

I did not expect to be moved by the flowers, but I was, and so was Lisa. As in the interviews with people in the queue, there was as much information to be gleaned about the mourners from these displays as there was about their thoughts on the late Queen. Clearly, from all the cards that included Paddington Bear hand in hand with the Queen, her recent and now world-famous clip of having tea at the palace with Paddington had resonated for a whole new generation. The ubiquitous bear's final words in the clip, after the hilarious account of Paddington and the Queen both boasting about their marmalade sandwiches, were on hundreds of cards throughout the park: "Thank you, ma'am . . . for *everything.*" The success of this sweet clip was proven by the desperate plea from the London Park Services for people who wanted to honour the late queen to not leave pots of marmalade or, worse, marmalade sandwiches amidst all the flowers.

People were visibly touched by these cards and flowers and despite the excited, almost bucolic atmosphere of the crowds, there was also a profound stillness as people approached the ever-expanding mounds. The ancient trees with their gnarled branches and sturdy trunks lent a strong solemnity to the scene.

At the same time, I got a measure of the pickle the CTV executives who fired Lisa were in from the number of Canadians who came up to her to tell her how wonderful she was, how much they supported her, and to ask if she was broadcasting the funeral for anyone. I enjoyed being her aide-de-camp, restricting overeager fans from closing in on her all at once. I felt a kinship with the people in the nearby palace deployed to do the same thing for their leading lady over the past seventy years.

\* \* \*

The other big assignment I had given myself for this day was to make a very special delivery St. James's Palace, not far from Green Park. St. James's, again, is a working palace, the principal seat of the Royal Court, and the site where Charles I, II, and III all made their commitments to rule faithfully and justly, one way or another. It is where all foreign ambassadors are officially accredited and where Anne, the Princess Royal, has her London residence. An extraordinary jumble of buildings, it also includes offices of the Royal Household and, in some of its out-of-the-way corners, storage space for the ornate uniforms of the Gentlemen Ushers with their vast golden epaulettes. Which is to say that St. James's is at once both a grand palace and a poky royal attic where the lesser accoutrements of monarchy are stored to await their periodic need.

It is also where the most important of several Chapels Royal is located and this was where I was headed. I had an important delivery to make, thanks to a remarkable connection through the small chapel at the University of Toronto college where I was the head (the title used to be "master" but is now "principal") for two

53

decades. It was during that time that the Queen was petitioned by the college to have the designation of our small chapel transformed into one of her three Chapels Royal in Canada. This is a really interesting tale, not widely known.

The original Chapel Royal, and this is going back well before Henry VIII's reign, was comprised of a number of priests and choristers who would travel with the sovereign wherever he was on the move around the country. Henry wanted a more permanent arrangement, so spaces were carved out of the expanses of two remarkable new edifices: St. James's Palace in London and Hampton Court Palace in Richmond on the River Thames. In time, these chapels were joined by a few other, all designated as Chapels Royal, including one in the Tower of London (possibly for occasional royal visitors under arrest).

All three Chapels Royal in Canada are associated with Indigenous nations. The first two celebrate the relationship between the sovereign and the Mohawk nation, allies going back to the reign of Queen Anne, while the third, the one I know best because I was one of the petitioners to the Queen for the change in status, was the Chapel of St. Catherine's at Massey College, University of Toronto. It was granted this honour because of its relationship to the Mississaugas of the Credit First Nation and it was a gesture on the part of the Queen to assist in an extraordinary commitment toward reconciliation between the Indigenous nations in Canada and the settler communities that had caused them such grief over the years. There has been so much tragedy in this relationship that the healing process now under way will take many more years to play out, but it has started and one of the small steps along the way is trying to build back bridges to a relationship of trust and mutual help that marked some of the earliest interactions. It was my hope that the symbolism of the redesignated chapel would in a small way help in the crucial business of reconciliation. To have the Queen herself approve the redesignation was a major step. As the Mississauga's eloquent chief Stacey LaForme said at the time of the rededication of the chapel in 2017:

> My people's ancestors were at Niagara when the Silver Covenant Chain of Friendship was extended into these lands over 250 years ago. It is in the spirit of that gathering that this chapel will serve as a place to gather regularly for this and future generations.
>
> Confederation set aside our treaty relationships, beginning a very dark chapter in the relationships between Indigenous and non-Indigenous peoples on these lands. The establishment of this Chapel Royal, a space to reflect, learn and reconnect, by Her Majesty and the Massey community 150 years later is a profound act of reconciliation. It will become, in effect, a new council fire for our peoples to gather around in love and friendship.

All of this is to explain why I was on a mission to bring sacred tobacco, grown especially on land set aside for both the Mohawk and Mississauga nations and their respective Chapels Royal, to the chief Chapel Royal at St. James's Palace and its Sub Dean, the Reverend Paul Wright. It was our luck that years earlier, Father Paul had done part of his training for the priesthood in Cree territory in Northern Manitoba. When the Queen asked him what he thought of the Massey College petition, he said he thought it was a good idea. I don't know for sure, but I believe that clinched it, and in any event this good priest has remained a loyal and inspiring friend ever since. I was about to task him with taking three gifts of sacred tobacco, blessed at the Canadian chapels, to present to the new

King. I had been invited into the palace and the chapel to make the initial presentation and lay the tobacco on the altar where it would rest until handed over to King Charles later in the month.

This I did, and the sacred tobacco was received with reverence and appreciation by Father Paul. As well, I was invited back for the next Sunday, the day before the state funeral, to attend a service with the Royal Household and see the tobacco safely ensconced on the altar. On this particular visit, I wanted to check out something I vaguely thought I remembered from my first visit the year before. I was looking for something lurking within the extraordinary "folds" of the ornately designed chapel ceiling, heavily embossed with royal insignia and armorial what-nots. Some of the fine detail was painted by Hans Holbein, the artist whose portraits came to define the Tudor eras of Henry VIII, Mary I, Edward VI, and Elizabeth I; other parts were quite contemporary. It took me a little time to locate my vaguely remembered quarry, but despite a stiff neck made stiffer by straining upward, I got my "eureka" moment. There, nestled near the organ pipes, was a sweet depiction of the head of a Welsh corgi. And not just any old corgi, but, I was told, one of the Queen's favourites, and it wasn't snarling or barking or nipping at anyone's ankles. It was just a corgi content with its lot in life, content with its place in the saga of the nation, just like her mistress.

# DAY 9, FRIDAY, SEPTEMBER 16

The queue was now threatening to go beyond four miles and had become its own international story, along with the cascading floral tributes and the renewed calls for people to resist leaving pots of marmalade. The King, having begun in Scotland and then been to Northern Ireland, headed off to Wales, the principality he had just handed over to his son and heir, Prince William. We know, if only (for some of us) from the ubiquitous series *The Crown* that Charles made a sincere effort to learn Welsh prior to becoming its prince in 1958 and his subsequent investiture in 1969. He used this particular skill adroitly this day when he addressed the Welsh parliament in the native tongue. Apparently, far more crucially, he was able to sign the guest book at an earlier encounter at Llandaff Cathedral with *his own unleaky pen.* The world gave a huge sigh of relief.

\* \* \*

Back in London, your intrepid reporter headed off to Canada House in Trafalgar Square to talk to the Canadian High Commissioner, the Honourable Ralph Goodale. He had already had three encounters with the new King, two were pro forma (the Accession Council, and after the address to Parliament), but one was substantive, or at least as substantive as the much called-upon monarch was capable of summoning during this week of non-stop encounters in which he tried to cover as many bases as he could.

Canada is the senior of the "overseas" realms and the Royal Family has always paid due consideration to that reality. Mr. Goodale is a down-to-earth politico from Saskatchewan who is an almost perfect representative of mainstream Canada. But he is also from a province that before too many more years will be unique in the country in that a majority of its residents will be Indigenous. He said he felt a strong sense that this King at this particular juncture in Canada's history was going to make a substantial difference not just in general reconciliation but also in understanding how the Crown can act as an effective bridge in the process, which is neither easy nor painless. "He's a good man," reported the High Commissioner. "I think we're lucky to have him as our King. You know he's been to Saskatchewan quite a few times and he always made a good impression. And I believe strongly he can help Canadians in the process of reconciliation. He's the right man at the right time."

It seemed a good note on which to finish the only quiet day of the week.

# DAY 10, SATURDAY SEPTEMBER, 17

The queue is now officially a full five miles long and thanks to the seasonable weather there is no sign of it waning, although it must, at some point, because the casket will be gone in thirty-six hours or so. I'm left to my own devices today, so I go hunting down some byways and obscure corners for royal curiosities. One of the best is the library at the Reform Club where I settle in to read some vintage publications. I know what I'm looking for and I know why. I wanted to see how the death of King George V was handled in 1936, how the abdication of King Edward VIII was reported (or papered over), and how the accession of King George VI unfolded. The reason it is important is that on one special moment in my life I did have a real conversation with Queen Elizabeth and it has haunted me ever since and, thanks to Prince Harry and his Meghan, the memory of it has become more haunting.

But first ponder this bit of reportage in the special coverage of the accession of King George VI in *The Sphere*, one of the more popular of the British weekly magazines in the first half of the twentieth century. Keep in mind that all during the lead-up to the abdication of Edward VIII at the end of 1936, the British media had embraced the cone of silence. It was U.S. and continental media that had a field day reporting on Edward's relationship with the twice-divorced Mrs. Wallis Warfield Simpson. Hardly a hint and nary a word emerged in the British media. As if to reinforce this willing acquiescence, *The Sphere* became practically lyrical as it noted the British reticence in dealing with the former King's love life:

> The constitutional crisis is over. We begin to emerge from what will seem to us to have been a nightmare of Ruritania. King Edward has decided. The long days of his agony of indecision are over and he has decided to sign away his divine right and glorious destiny for what seems to him today at once the best for his individual happiness and Mrs. Simpson's, and the honourable and patriotic course to take. Let no man dare to cast a stone of criticism. Every sane man will cry aloud for silence and amnesty. Our most sacred beliefs and intimacies have for weeks been the peep-show of civilization and we offer our profound gratitude to all the responsible institutions and Press organs which have so generously and honourably exercised restraint which decency requires; all who have resisted a rich occasion for commercializing a private tragedy. Those, especially Britons, who did not resist the temptation, we shall not easily forgive.

Despite this encomium of praise for restraint and holding back any *J'accuse* gutter journalism, *The Sphere* nevertheless adjusts its vantage point to indulge in a little bit of non-resistance for what, in the end, was exactly a rich occasion:

> King Edward's outstanding qualities need no further stressing. His outstanding weakness was in his choice of friends, in his judgment of character and of what was seemly for one in his

position. He could not see that as Prince and King his private affairs must be directed by the same standards as his public duties.

The "Instrument of Abdication" was signed in King Edward's Windsor residence, a charming and far from vast country home called Fort Belvedere. It's actually a faux fort with a line of decorative cannons, all spiked, which was predominantly constructed in the Gothic Revival style in 1820 and has been used by members of the Royal Family, or their friends, ever since. Windsor Castle is just a few miles away. Fort Belvedere was King Edward VIII's favourite residence and you can hear his longing for it in some of the interviews he gave following his abdication and his demotion to Duke of Windsor. Today, its leasehold is held by the Weston family, although the freehold remains in the sovereign's Crown Estate. The Westons are elegant storekeepers on both sides of the Atlantic: in Canada, family members own a range of merchandise emporiums from glitzy Holt Renfrew to egalitarian Loblaws and Shoppers Drug Mart. In England, their holdings included Selfridges (recently sold by the family for around $5.3 billion) and the very swish Fortnum & Mason with several outlets, the most famous of which is on Piccadilly Avenue in London. The Weston family members are known for keeping low profiles and for generosity thanks to their fortunes. Galen Weston and his wife, Hilary, have been the current occupants of Fort Belvedere for some years and they have been both neighbours and friends of the Queen and Prince Philip. In just a short period of time, three of this foursome have died: the Queen, Prince Philip, and Galen Weston. Mrs. Weston was also a former Lieutenant Governor of Ontario, which, in the Westminster parliamentary system, meant she was in effect the Queen's "regent" in Canada's most populous province. Shy by nature, she did a superb job and followed the lead of the Queen in most respects, especially in avoiding controversy in the political realm.

Nowadays, Hilary is literally the only one of the foursome left holding the Fort. It was in her honour, a few years back, that her family gave her a spectacular birthday party at Fort Belvedere to which the Queen and Prince Philip came. As a working member of the press who often covered royal tours or events, I had had anodyne exchanges with the Queen. It was here at Mrs. Weston's celebrated birthday party that I had the only substantive conversation I've had with Her Majesty, one of about several hundred thousand short conversations she had in her career. In fact, it might be more than a million, all of them instantly forgotten. But for me, as for each person who got more than a "where have you come from," it was an exchange to be cherished and retained to the grave.

After an elegant reception for the Canadian guests inside Fort Belvedere itself, everyone was ushered into one of the several event tents set up outside for dinner, after which there was a display of fireworks accompanied by the string section of the London Philharmonic Orchestra (I did stress that this was a significant birthday party and perhaps I should also add that members of Cirque du Soleil were performing acrobatics in the neighbouring trees all floodlit for the occasion). We were watching from a special viewing gallery outside the dining tents and my wife, Elizabeth, and I pushed a bit to get to the front of the crowd so we could have a good view. Once situated, Elizabeth looked to see who was on my other side and then whispered in my ear: "Do you know who we are standing beside?" I did. Obviously I did. I had conspired to be standing there. "Good evening, Your Majesty," I said. "I hope you are enjoying all this as much as we are."

"Thank you," she said, turning slightly to see who had addressed her so directly. "Are you from Canada?"

"Yes, ma'am," I said, and then, to keep things anodyne, I asked her how old she was when she first visited Fort Belvedere.

"Oh I was young. Margaret and I would be invited over by my uncle and we had the run of the place. It was so exciting. There was no protocol at all and he had the first outdoor heated swimming pool in England. It was magic here."

"I read somewhere that you were his favourite niece."

"Oh, that's not fair to Margaret. She was so young then. She never got a chance to know him when she was older . . ."

The Queen paused for a moment here. Then she looked at me very straight on and said: "It was a very great tragedy, you know. Very great."

And then an enormous barrage of fireworks went off and it was impossible to carry on a conversation and by the time things quietened down the moment had been lost. After the barrage, someone behind us said: "I wonder what the neighbours are going to say!" and the Queen laughed out loud. "That's very funny," she said, and I couldn't get our conversation back to where it had ended.

I can only speculate. I don't think she meant that it was "a very great tragedy" that King Edward VIII never got to know Princess Margaret better. I think it was a very great tragedy because Edward had been so popular as Prince of Wales and people had been keen to identify with him when he ascended to the throne. I think she also thought it was a tragedy because her own shy, stammering but hugely beloved father had to take over and the pressures (pressures and cigarettes) almost certainly led to his early death, in his fifties. I think she thought it was a tragedy because she was required at far too young an age to assume the burden of her destiny when she might have preferred to lead the quiet life of a countryside British aristocrat untroubled by affairs of state, or at least not to have had the mantle of sovereignty thrust on her shoulders at such a young age and just a few years after she had married.

That conversation haunted me as the Harry and Meghan drama unfolded a few years later. Talk about understudies! Harry had garnered about the same amount of public affection and enthusiastic support as that great-uncle had. Meghan, the American divorcee, like Mrs. Simpson, has already managed in a short time to attract about the same amount of venom and contempt, and has also been responsible for her Prince eschewing his royal destiny. It's a remake of an old family drama: "Abdication: The Sequel."

I believe the Queen saw the potential for a second tragedy and had tried hard to incorporate Meghan into the Royal Family and the round of royal duties, but it didn't work, and maybe it never could have. We are looking at a cultural disconnect of monumental proportions: "Carry on Regardless" versus "Me, Myself, and My Boy." Who needs a sixth season of *The Crown* when Harry and his bride can provide everything needed, and for pretty low production costs.

# DAY 11, SUNDAY, SEPTEMBER 18

Although this was supposed to be the day of rest, officially ordered since the proclamation of the Ten Commandments, the Reverend Paul Wright, Sub Dean of the Chapel Royal at St. James's Palace, was not able to take the day off. First of all he was a priest doing God's business on God's day and that meant presiding at a Eucharist in the chapel for members of the Royal Household, a Eucharist minus the extraordinary choir of the Chapel Royal. The choir was dispatched to be incorporated into the funeral choral ensemble at Westminster Abbey at the same hour for a final rehearsal. It is a traditional Anglican choir: men and boys or, in local parlance, "Gentlemen of the Chapel Royal" singing low and the "Children of the Chapel Royal" singing high. The historical list of organists and choirmasters is extraordinary if you know and value anything of the choral tradition: Thomas Tallis, William Byrd, John Blow, Jeremiah Clark, William Croft, Orlando Gibbons, Henry Purcell, William Boyce. But on this day, there was only an organist and a hymn sung enthusiastically if not exactly luminously.

Although small—it can only hold about 150 people, including the choir—the Royal Chapel exudes a strong sense of history. The heart of Queen Mary I (Henry VIII's eldest daughter) is buried below the choir stalls. It was here that Queen Elizabeth I came to pray as she awaited messages of the progress and fate of the Spanish Armada. This was also the place where King Charles I knelt in prayer on the last morning of his life and took Holy Communion before being led to a nearby specially constructed scaffolding for his execution. And it remains a special place for today's Royal Family. It was here that Prince Louis, youngest child of William and Catherine, was baptized.

It is also here that the gift of sacred tobacco from two North American Indigenous nations was resting discreetly behind one of the altar candlesticks, awaiting its presentation to King Charles III. And as I sat and knelt in prayer in this extraordinary room on this Sunday morning, the day before the most extraordinary funeral of our time, it struck me that something important was happening beyond the funeral itself, something of a correction to history only achievable through the good graces of royalty and Indigenous forbearance and forgiveness and this, too, requires a continuation of this particular tale.

In 1710, during the reign of Queen Anne, four Indigenous leaders, known at the time as "The Four Kings of Canada," made the perilous trip from North America to England. Actually, five had set off but one of their number died en route. Three were Mohawk chiefs and a fourth was a Mohican leader from the Algonquin nation. They were received as heads of their nations and accorded full head-of-state ceremonies, transported to St. James's Palace in official coaches and received by the Queen. Gifts were exchanged, including sacred tobacco. Some of the great officers of state were in attendance. What was everyone really up to? What was the *realpolitik* of the moment? Simple. It was a treaty and an alliance between the British Crown and these nations, inevitably against the French in Quebec.

The Mohawk nation has remained loyal to the Crown ever since. Initially, in their ancestral lands in what is now upstate New

York, they stayed loyal during the American Revolution when, like all Loyalists in the new republic, they had to hightail it quickly to Canada to escape tarring and feathering or, in the Indigenous peoples' case, annihilation. That is how the Mohawk nation came to be honoured by having two of their places of worship in Canada designated Chapels Royal. Our third Chapel Royal, in Toronto at Massey College, was a johnny-come-lately but it, too, came with the same sense of sharing and commitment to friendship and reconciliation. This summoning of ancient (and for ages largely forgotten or eschewed) covenants is misunderstood still in Canada. One of the great hopes is that this new King will continue and extend the practices of his mother, for whom Crown-Indigenous relations were always a part of every "homecoming" she made to Canada.

In June 2019, a historic gathering took place at the Chapel Royal at Massey College. The National Indigenous Chief Perry Bellegarde made an extraordinary address inside the chapel to the Governor General and all the other representatives of the Queen in Canada: the Lieutenant Governors of the province, and the territorial commissioners from the high north. The message was both profound and simple. For too long, Chief Bellegarde told the assembled vice regal representatives of the Crown, both our institutions have been taken for granted and thought powerless, both the Indigenous peoples and the ceremonial representatives of the Queen. In fact, Bellegarde argued, it was the opposite. "We have much we can do together to teach the importance of protecting the gifts of land the Creator bequeathed us." The Lieutenant Governor of Ontario reiterated the point: "There is so much that we all must do, but particularly those of us with a platform, if we are going to continue to be resilient in the years ahead."

That was in 2019. Two years later, in his final visit as Prince of Wales, Charles made reconciliation the key element in his "homecoming" to Canada and gave a strong hint what his priorities would be when he became king. That was why these small gifts of tobacco, awaiting delivery on the high altar of his premier Chapel Royal carried such significance. They symbolized the effort to start telling a better story than the one that had been told for a century and a half in Canada, of forced assimilation and cultural malfeasance. It is an effort to return to the implied relation of equals when the Four Kings of Canada parlayed with the Queen at St. James's Palace.

It was with thoughts like this that some of us emerged into the courtyard outside the chapel, and it was those thoughts that carried our prayers and petitions as we gathered in London for the solemn day that was to follow: we were solemn, but grateful for the life and reign of the late Queen; solemn, but hopeful for the life and reign of the new King.

# DAY 12, MONDAY, SEPTEMBER 19

In the early hours before one of these great occasions of state, London is wonderfully eerie. It helps to have a press pass to take in the atmosphere because you can move about with a certain amount of freedom. Security is beyond intense but, being British, is rather carefully camouflaged. The crucial area encompassed Parliament and Westminster Hall and Westminster Abbey. Everything within this perimeter, along the River Thames, was formally described by security personnel as "sterile." In other words, nothing budges without ID, except birds, and even then you have to have the right sort of ID. You can't go more than a few steps without someone politely checking you out. Atop all the surrounding buildings, armed personnel have been on duty for days, and on this morning of mornings, when the full panoply of state will be on display with most of the world's leaders in attendance, you can intuit the security intensity, although you don't really feel it as oppressive. It's a British gift born of experience with these sorts of magnificent events.

The last of the public have filed past the sarcophagus in the hall by 6:30 a.m., and because the hundreds of thousands were all individually tagged with wrist IDs, officials knew exactly who the last people would be and by what time they would arrive and how long they would take to walk through the hall, so there were no disappointed late arrivals complaining at the entrance. In a previous funeral, for the Queen Mother, I had got media identification to cover the event for a Toronto newspaper and I managed to linger in Westminster Hall till the very end. On that occasion, there were huge crowds, too, about half the number for her daughter, also patiently queuing. Then, the great hall also glimmered in the soft light which nevertheless caught the twinkling of the jewels of the Queen Consort's smaller crown on her coffin.

At the end of that earlier occasion, it was unbelievably peaceful in that extraordinary space and the two or three of us who had conspired to be the last commented as we left that it had been a very special moment— metaphysical, really, and maybe even spiritual. Architecture, history, panoply, and a due sense of an ordered drama had all conspired to have their effect. According to media coverage, it was the same atmosphere this morning as the final people left Westminster Hall, and the state together with the state church took over the coffin for the final two stages of this spectacular drama: the actual funeral at Westminster Abbey at 11:00 a.m., and the subsequent trip to Windsor Castle and the interment in the royal crypt below St. George's Chapel.

Those lucky enough to gain entrance to Westminster Abbey started arriving by 8:00 a.m. I say "lucky" blithely. If you are trying to keep a grip on the big picture, about the worst place to find yourself is stuck in a seat behind a pillar in the Abbey where they are reluctant to so much as allow you a "health break." Far better to have a media pass and be roaming. For most of those who did have a *laissez-passer* into the Abbey, it would be a long wait, over three hours, but then again not nearly as long or as cold as the wait in the queue. Once you are in the Abbey, there is a kind of imposed humility established ahead of time, thanks to seating arrangements. And the humility was imposed not only on the ordinary invitees, but also on most visiting heads of state and heads of government. Virtually all of them were required to arrive in one of the special buses without their outriders or flunkies. The one exception was President Joseph Biden and his wife, Jill, who managed to come in their own car—one can imagine the to-ing and fro-ing this entailed between respective security services—but then in a seeming effort to make sure the president didn't get too uppity, the "First Couple" were smartly escorted to the fourteenth row, toward the back of the east aisle, significantly behind Canada's Justin Trudeau who himself was behind Canada's first-ever Indigenous Governor General, Mary Simon. The logic was simple: Trudeau is the head of government of a "realm" of which the Queen (now the King) was head of state (two points in the seating game), but in Canada the Governor General represented Herself for all practical purposes and formally, at least, was her designated regent (three points and a trumping of the PM). It was the same for the other fourteen realms.

Biden gets only one point, even though he is both head of state and head of a government. Perhaps the Americans shouldn't have had their revolution, after all. Ironists have noted that with their rigid constitution forged in the eighteenth century, they ended up creating a head of state modeled on the Hanoverian system and seem constantly to be re-electing George III to the White House, but irony wasn't sufficient to get President and Jill Biden any closer to the Queen's coffin. Nor would Donald Trump have fared any better because the Queen liked him more. As she herself would have said: "*Really!*"

In the very front rows of this gilded section were the reigning sovereigns of over a dozen remaining monarchies. Queen Margrethe of Denmark was in the prime position, directly across from King Charles with only the sarcophagus intervening. It was noted quietly that she had succeeded her cousin Elizabeth not only as the longest reigning current head of state and but also as the only remaining "queen regnant." Two days later it was further announced she had contracted COVID during the event. The funeral turned out to be a bit of a spreader.

The next few hours, for some, were fascinating. Every single member of the two thousand who got inside had been assigned to a specific group in a specific area of the Abbey, with specific arrival times and with specific instructions to stay put. This included even the lesser family members. Remarkably, and for the first time in years, Sarah, Duchess of York, was welcomed back to the fold. She is the divorced spouse but live-in partner of Prince Andrew, the son who has done so much to cloud the final years of his mother's reign with disgrace. She had apparently won her former mother-in-law's heart through her loyalty to dogs and to the miscreant son. This, too, is part of the historic drama of monarchy. It is, in the end, a family, full of the dysfunctions every family experiences from time to time.

The funeral service itself unfolded perfectly, as intended. It's what is expected with the sort of clockwork precision one relies upon for these occasions and in these settings. If you could have taken a metaphysical vantage point high above the proceedings, with an ability to swoop down and observe its particularities, the strongest impression you would be left with was the genius of advance planning. That's what makes it so compelling to watch, symbolized by the crack team of eight Guardsmen who transported their royal "burden" so movingly despite the crisp discipline. Taken from its catafalque in Westminster Hall and placed on the same gun carriage which had carried Elizabeth's great-great-grandmother Queen Victoria at her 1901 funeral, naval ratings were similarly deployed to carry and brake it fore and aft. Military bearing at this funeral was one of the most salient features of the processions, and it filtered down to all the non-military guests, who instinctively carried on with their own military gaits.

Leading the parade, again, were members of the Royal Canadian Mounted Police, yet another reminder to all who were watching that the Queen's realms extended beyond Great Britain (if getting less "great" by the nanosecond under the new government of Prime Minister Liz Truss, entrusted with the care of the ancient kingdom just days before in one of the last official acts by the living and animated woman whose body was now being borne so movingly). It was often noted this day that the late Queen herself, and the trail of history enshrouded with her inside the coffin, was the only identifiable entity justifying the word *great* by the end of her reign.

Walking behind the gun carriage were her four children, King Charles, Princess Anne the Princess Royal, Prince Andrew the Bad, and Prince Edward the dutiful. Behind them came Prince William, the new Prince of Wales; Prince Harry the Bolter; and plain Mr. Peter Phillips. This is a real family, after all, putting on a good show. The troubles of Harry, and the embarrassment of Andrew: these things haven't gone away. They have been mitigated somewhat by the overwhelming magnitude of the events during which they are expected to carry on regardless, but the challenges they both represent to the Royal Family have not disappeared and it will be now be the responsibility of the new King to manage them. He and they will be watched. *Closely.* It could be described as the downside, or cost, of privilege.

The funeral service that ensued, from the stately procession down the main aisle of the Abbey through the music and sermon and readings and prayers were Christian in focus, via the Church of England, although other denominations participated at appointed moments. But what gave the solemnity such a heightened aspect was the sense that it was so closely tied to the Queen's own faith, which we know was straightforward, direct, and, in its essence, simple. She believed that the arrival of Jesus Christ on earth set an example of service and duty and sacrifice and in her own way she tried to honour His message in the role destiny had bequeathed her. Look again at the particularities of the service, all of which she either ordered up personally or were suggestions she had approved:

The hymn from the 23rd Psalm of the Jewish scriptures, "The Lord's My Shepherd," was sung at her wedding to Prince Philip three quarters of a century earlier.

The oldest member of her family, the Duke of Kent, walked as a young teenager at the funeral of her father, King George, in 1952. Inside the Abbey today, he was sitting in a chair quite close to nine-year-old Prince George and seven-year-old Princess Charlotte, second and third in line to the throne after their father, the new Prince of Wales.

Atop the coffin, perhaps even more symbolic than the crown, orb, and sceptre, was an extraordinary wreath of flowers picked from three gardens: at Buckingham Palace, Clarence House, and King Charles's favourite residence, Highgrove Park. The flowers were chosen, as the Queen knew they would be, by the King himself who had his own up-and-down relationship with his mother (and also with flowers as he was alleged to have once talked to tulips). She had kept the throne safe for him to occupy and spared him what she hadn't herself been spared: a life in the constitutional straitjacket she had worn from the age of twenty-six when the Crown had been placed on her head at almost the same spot where her body now lay. The flowers in the wreath were their own kind of poetry: roses and pelargoniums, hydrangea and sedum, dahlias and scabious, all embedded in clusters of English moss and oak branches. In the press, handouts given to journalists covering the funeral, it was noted that the wreath also contained sprigs of myrtle grown from a sprig that was part of her bridal bouquet when she married Prince Philip, also—*also,* again and again—at almost the same spot in the Abbey.

The procession of the funeral cortège down the main aisle of the Abbey, with Croft's hauntingly somber "Funeral Sentences" being sung by the joint choirs of the Abbey and the Chapel Royal at St. James's Palace re-created once again the whole notion of the dignity of a monarchical state, however reduced in its political power. Ceremonial power, always underestimated, nevertheless has at key moments remarkable emotional suasion and no more so than right here as the procession made its identical route back up to the sanctuary where the young Elizabeth had been crowned. The entrances and exits of kings and queens are themselves moments of state just as much as they are personal. Do you have to be a royal romantic like me to be moved by these proximities? Maybe, but I feel sorry for those who don't get it. It must be like people who think opera is all about the plot and the music is merely incidental.

Well, maybe it's not all romantic. This is a human drama, after all, and it struck me as remarkable that this was the first funeral of a British sovereign to be held in Westminster Abbey since that of King George II in 1760. All the subsequent ones were held at St. George's Chapel at Windsor Castle. George was the second Hanoverian and that funeral had been memorable for other reasons than ceremonial drama, as described hilariously by Horace Walpole, the fourth Earl of Orford. He wrote to a friend in 1760:

Do you know, I had the curiosity to go to the burying t'other night; I had never seen a royal funeral. Nay, I walked as a rag of quality, which I found would be, and so it was, the easiest way of seeing it. It is absolutely a noble sight. The Prince's Chamber hung with purple and a quantity of silver lamps, the coffin under a canopy of purple velvet, and six vast chandeliers of silver on high stands had a very good effect: the ambassador from Tripoli and his son were carried in to see the chamber. The procession through a line of foot-guards, every seventh man bearing a torch, the horse-guards lining the outside, their officers with drawn sabres and crepe sashes, on horseback, the drums muffled, the fifes, bells tolling and minute guns, all this was very solemn. But the charm was the entrance of the Abbey, where we were received by the Dean and chapter in rich copes, the choir and almsmen all bearing torches; the while Abbey so illuminated, that one saw it to greater advantage than at day; the tombs, long aisles, and fretted roof all appearing distinctly, and with the happiest chiaroscuro. There wanted nothing but incense, and little chapels here and therewith priests saying mass for the repose of the defunct—yet one could not complain of its not being catholic enough . . . When we came to the Chapel of Henry VII all solemnity and decorum ceased—no order was observed, people sat or stood where they could or would, the yeomen of the guard were crying out for help, oppressed by the immense weight of the coffin, the Bishop read sadly, and blundered in the prayers, the fine chapter, "Man that is born of woman," was chanted not read, and the anthem, besides being unmeasurably tedious, would have served as well for a nuptial. The real serious part was the figure of the Duke of Cumberland (King George's youngest son), heightened by a thousand melancholy circumstances. He had a dark brown Adonis (wig) and a cloak of black cloth with a train of five yards. Attending the funeral of his father, however little reason he had to love him, could not be pleasant. His leg extremely bad, yet forced to stand upon it near two hours, his face bloated and distorted with his late paralytic stroke, which has affected too one of his eyes, and placed over the mouth of the vault, to which in all probability he must himself so descend—think how unpleasant a situation! He bore it all with a firm and unaffected countenance. The grave scene was fully contrasted by the burlesque of the Duke of Newcastle—he fell into a fit of crying the moment he came into the chapel and flung himself back in the stall, the Archbishop hovering over him with a smelling bottle—but in two minutes his curiosity got the better of his hypocrisy and he ran about the chapel with his glass to spy who was or was not there, spying with one hand and mopping his brow with t'other. Then returned the fear of catching cold, and the Duke of Cumberland, who was sinking with heat, felt himself weighed down, and turning round, found it was the Duke of Newcastle standing upon his train to avoid the chill of the marble.

\* \* \*

At the funeral of King George II's descendant, there were also two dukes caught out. Andrew, Duke of York, and Harry, Duke of Sussex, who seemed visibly out of joint. Andrew had lost his greatest defender and it was generally assumed he would soon be thrown to the wolves, one way or another. And Harry looked for all the world like a lost boy, clutching the hand of the woman he loved and looking out of sorts in the very setting in which he once shone so engagingly and brightly. That true love of his, Meghan Markle, now a duchess, looked for all the world like the successor to that earlier wannabe duchess, Mrs. Simpson, who had weaned her man, the King-Emperor Edward VIII, from his throne. At least Meghan hasn't been able to cause a constitutional crisis. At least not yet.

It is not inappropriate, even at this solemn juncture, to point out how decisive the old Queen was in handling the two of them, much as she clearly adored them. Andrew, allegedly the favourite of her offspring, had brought shame to the family through his association with the American millionaire and "fixer" Jeffrey Epstein, and the accusations that the duke had had sex with a teenage girl pimped by Epstein. Pretty ugly stuff. He can't travel to the United States without fear of being served with a notice of contempt of court and arrested. The notoriety has cost his family at least US$12 million in payments to the claimant, who Andrew stoutly maintains he never met, and this, despite a damning photograph, caused the famous eighteenth-century children's poem to be updated, from:

*Oh, the Grand old Duke of York,*
*He had ten thousand men,*
*He marched them up to the top of the hill*
*And he marched him down again*

To:

*Oh the Grand old Duke of York,*
*He had 12 million quid,*
*He gave it to someone he never met,*
*For something he never did.*

Favourite or not, the Queen stripped him of his royal duties and patronages. She did not abandon him entirely and made a point of having him as her escort at the memorial the previous May for Prince Philip, but she didn't hesitate to leave his disgrace underlined. She loved him, as she showed, but he was not going to be allowed to shake the monarchy any more than he already had.

The trouble with Harry was different. The prince and his celebrity wife had it all worked out that they could drop in and out of royal life as they pleased. At least, they had it worked out until they came up against the Queen's steely resolve that the choice wasn't theirs, it was hers, and her iron-clad rule was that you were either in the Royal Family or you were not, and by making the choice they did, they were expelled. End of saga. It didn't mean she didn't love them. It didn't mean she wouldn't see them. It just meant that officially they were out of the picture. Both Andrew and Harry probably felt blindsided, so secure were they in their sense of the reciprocated affection they had for their mother and grandmother. Neither had really taken stock of her rigid protection of the monarchy, by word and deed. And you could see it on their faces throughout the obsequies honouring her unique and unsullied definition of a life of service and duty.

Typically, the couple who have done no wrong, who have held the fort and are now set on a well laid-out journey for the rest of their lives, Prince William and his Kate, formerly the Duke and Duchess of Cambridge, newly minted by the King as the Prince and Princess of Wales, remained dutifully out of the headlines. William is in the great mould of the Royal House of Windsor's sweet dullards, ditto for beautiful Kate. It's why they will be fine as King and Queen one day, just as was William's great-grandfather, the sweet dullard George VI, and also his great-great-grandfather the not-quite-so-sweet George V (whose greatest passion was not Queen Mary, his wife, but his stamp collection, which mostly featured his own image on stamps from the constituent parts of the far-flung empire).

The actual day-to-day job of sovereign, regardless of how much you want to indulge fantasies of castles and Crown jewels and great state occasions, is tedious beyond grief. It needs a solemn sense of service and duty and the single-minded pursuit of an ideal of intuitive leadership (one that scarcely needs to be understood to be followed). William has learned this ideal directly from his grandmother, both by example and also at all those private lunches she had with him in the last years of her life. As for Kate, she is gaining in confidence both in her ability to speak the genial inanities her fate requires of her, but also to echo the glamour that was the hallmark of her late mother-in-law, the absent but ever-looming Princess Diana.

Throughout all the days of official mourning. the two of them played their roles to perfection, never once causing a flutter of anxiety, always wearing the appropriate uniform or mourning gear. This was set beside Harry and Meghan, holding hands whenever possible for the cameras to see, and grousing over when he was or was not allowed, as an unofficial royal, to wear a uniform. It was pointed out by more than one observer that since Harry and his wicked uncle, Andrew, were the only members of the family who had actually seen active wartime service in the military, it was arch and mean-spirited of the new King and his advisers to limit their use of uniforms. Like others, I thought it was appropriate. Regardless of battlefield experience, they had both failed in the more demanding task of protecting their family and the ancient institution of monarchy from public and official opprobrium.

The Abbey service itself was both moving and predictable, or at least predictable to anyone who is familiar with the great state rites: procession, hymns, sermon, anthems, prayers, recessional. It's fairly unvarying and has been for a couple of centuries, the Duke of Newcastle's "hypocrisy" notwithstanding. If you look at old publications reporting on the funerals of the Queen's father, grandfather, great-grandfather, and great-great-grandmother, you will find most of the same elements revived for hers. Even King Charles's upcoming Coronation, with the crown which will be encrusted with some of the same jewels that were on display atop his mother's coffin, will follow a familiar pattern with the key elements of an anointing and a crowning and many, many vows of loyalty. These events are affecting precisely because of the human beings at the centre of the ceremony and because of the links to history and the projections into the future. If the monarchy survives into the twenty-second century, in all likelihood the Queen's great-grandson Prince George will remember something of the day Elizabeth the Great was buried and brood over his own funeral arrangements.

\* \* \*

The final act was the journey to Windsor Castle and the short service of committal and interment in St. George's Chapel, another of what is amusingly and officially known as "a royal peculiar," an ecclesiastical edifice under the direct control and favour of the reigning sovereign and not under the jurisdiction of the Church of England. It is also the spiritual home of the Knights of the Garter, the oldest and most senior chivalric order in the United Kingdom. Founded by King Edward III in 1348, it was inspired by the legends of King Arthur and the Knights of the Round Table, thus incorporating both legend and the politics of the day. The colourful outfits the knights and dames wear at their annual outing in Windsor can be traced right back to that fourteenth-century beginning. Inside the chapel, the armorial bearings of all the current and former knights grace the walls of the sanctuary, and knightly banners add immeasurably to its antique lustre. It is also the burial place of most of Queen Elizabeth's family and so the service here seemed personal, although it, too, followed a fairly rigid pattern with the rubric of the Anglican Book of Common Prayer. Hymns, prayers, anthems, and short homilies. It has often been reported how much the late Queen disliked wordy sermons. Once someone asked her favourite chaplain at St. James's Palace whether the Queen was "high church" or "low church" (meaning was she on the side of "catholic" or "evangelical" traditions within the Anglican church). He replied immediately: "Neither. She is for short church!"

Finally, as all the reigns of all the kings and queens of England must end, Elizabeth's chief herald, the Garter King of Arms, proclaimed her earthly "styles and titles":

> Thus it hath pleased Almighty God to take out of this transitory life unto His Divine Mercy the Most High, Most Mighty, and Excellent Monarch, Elizabeth the Second, by the Grace of God of the United Kingdom of Great Britain and Northern Ireland and Her other realms and Territories Queen, Head of the Commonwealth, Defender of the Faith, and Sovereign of the most Noble Order of the Garter.

In other words, *Sic transit Gloria mundi*: Thus passes the glory of the world.

* * *

"The pattern of many leaders is to be exalted in life and forgotten after death," intoned Justin Welby, the Archbishop of Canterbury, from the Abbey pulpit earlier in the day. "The pattern for all who serve God, famous or obscure, respected or ignored, is that death is the door to glory. Her late Majesty famously declared in a twenty-first-birthday broadcast that her whole life would be dedicated to serving the nation and the Commonwealth. Rarely has such a promise been so well kept."

The Archbishop also recalled the words the Queen had taken from a famous Second World War torch song sung by Vera Lynn: "Service in life, hope in death. All who follow the Queen's example, and inspiration of trust and faith in God, can with her say: 'We will meet again.'"

It is not a stretch to say that the Queen's faith may have equaled, if not surpassed, that of her archbishop who sometimes seemed appreciably more burdened than she by the stress of a publicly scrutinized role in national life. She was, as her husband once said of her, "forbearing to a fault," but she was also a stickler for protocol and timing and that was why she probably had more enjoyment over planning her own funeral than anyone else.

That it would end with two verses of "God Save the King" was as inevitable as the Last Post being sounded, along with the longest minute of silence ever heard in St. George's Chapel, at least within memory.

As she herself often observed, life is a series of arrivals and departures, but very few people in anyone's lifetime ever witnessed such an arrival and such a departure. In a speech following her Coronation in 1952, she identified with the drama in which she was the central character and drew from it what she thought was its essence as it concerned her relationship with the people whose destinies she had been asked to lead:

The ceremonies you have seen today are ancient, and some of their origins are veiled in the mists of the past. But their spirit and their meaning shine through the ages never, perhaps, more brightly than now. I have in sincerity pledged myself to your service, as so many of you have pledged to mine. Throughout all my life and with all my heart I shall strive to be worthy of that trust.

And so she did. And then some. Her final reward at the funeral came from the sweet laments two of her own regimental Pipe Majors offered at the end of the morning and afternoon services, the funeral first, and then as her coffin descended before the eyes of the world to the crypt she will now share with her husband, her sister, and her mother and father. The name of that lament set the signature on the whole twelve days of official and private mourning:

*Sleep dearie, sleep.*

# ACKNOWLEDGEMENTS

Robert Busikewicz

Communication officers of the Royal Household

Canadian High Commissioner to the U.K., Ralph Goodale

Hon. William Hepburne-Scott

Lisa LaFlamme

Elizabeth MacCallum

Andree Marin, Robertson Davies Library, Massey College

Lord Polwarth

Victoria Ribbans, Communications Office, Westminster Abbey

Anthony and Kit VanTullekan

Ken Whyte and the Sutherland House team

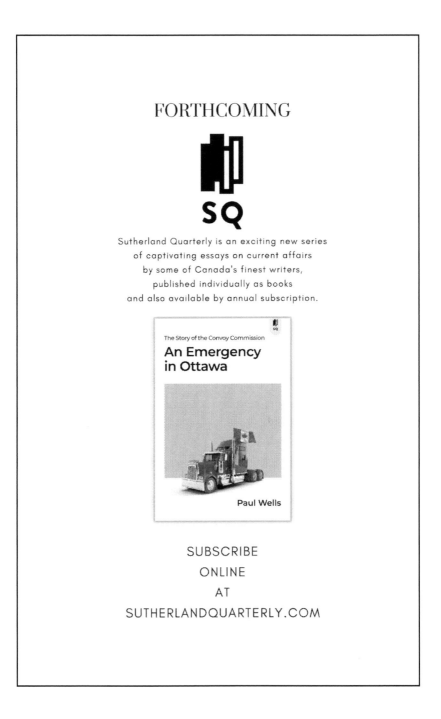

# GET THE <u>WHOLE</u> STORY

# GIVE A <u>THOUGHTFUL</u> GIFT

## DELIVERY & PAYMENT DETAILS

### Subscriber Info

NAME:
ADDRESS:
EMAIL:                                    PHONE:

### Payment Options

- Enclose a cheque or money order for $79.00 (includes HST) made out to Sutherland House Inc. Send to Sutherland House, 205-416 Moore Ave, Toronto, ON, Canada M4G 1C9
- Debit my Visa or MasterCard for $79.00 (includes HST)

CARD NUMBER: ____ ____ ____ ____        CVV: ___
EXPIRY DATE: __ / __                     AMOUNT: $
PURCHASER'S NAME:                        SIGNATURE:

OR SUBSCRIBE ONLINE AT SUTHERLANDQUARTERLY.COM